Does Jesus Make a Difference?

Proceedings of the College Theology Society

edited by Thomas M. McFadden

A CROSSROAD BOOK   *The Seabury Press* · *New York*

1974
The Seabury Press
815 Second Avenue, New York, N.Y. 10017

Copyright © 1974 by The Seabury Press, Inc.
Designed by Carol Basen
Printed in the United States of America

Library of Congress Cataloging in Publication Data

College Theology Society.
  Does Jesus make a difference?

  "A Crossroad book."
  "Twelve articles, originally delivered at the 1973
meeting of the College Theology Society."
  1. Jesus Christ—Person and offices—Congresses.
I. McFadden, Thomas M., ed.   II. Title.
BT202.C64 1974   232   73–17902
ISBN 0–8164–1151–4

Introduction

The question of Jesus making any difference has a distinctly modern ring to it. Christians have, of course, always been challenged to respond to Jesus' identity, and that response has been the very essence of faith. But the grounds of the issue, insofar as it is presented precisely as a theological problem, now seem to have shifted. The question has become "existential"—a shift entirely consonant with the contemporary emphasis on the subjective meaning and significance of the realities Christians have chosen to live by. Prior cultural configurations within which Christian faith could perform an integrative function seem to have broken up, and the new perspectives of our age call out for the synthetic capacities of a new theology.

This need to investigate the Christian faith critically becomes evident to anyone who spends much time in a college classroom. Hence the College Theology Society decided to set itself such a task at its 1973 convention in Philadelphia. This book represents some of the papers presented at that convention, and as such supplies abundant evidence of the intellectual vitality and seriousness of the Society's members.

The book is divided into three parts, the first of which outlines how Jesus' meaning was variously estimated within the history of Christianity, but especially during the time of New Testament composition. The implied argument which unites these four articles is that the radical shifts in articulating the meaning of Jesus throughout Christian history clearly allow for a similar process today.

The second part of the book is a positive statement on the difference that Jesus does in fact make. Jesus is seen as the unique mediator whose significance can be gauged only in the patterns of Christian life; as the horizon of man's dynamic orientation to the fullness of spirit; as the divine presence in our neighbor; and as the image of God's redeeming acceptance of sinful man. In part III, some specifically contemporary issues are raised and Jesus' bearing upon them explored. Speaking in tongues as a religious phenomenon often connected with Christian pentecostalism is examined from a theological/psychological perspective. The political repercussions of Jesus' message, even when one grants the apolitical content of Jesus' own preaching, is set forth. Finally, the understanding of Jesus as one who accepted death as the fulfillment of his existence is shown to have important significance in the light of modern man's concern over dying.

Since this study is, in a very real way, a product of the College Theology Society, its appearance reflects the leadership of the Society's Board of Directors, especially its national officers: Rev. Francis J. Buckley, S.J., of the University of San Francisco, President; Sister Vera Chester, C.S.J., of the College of St. Catherine, Vice-President; Sister Miriam Ward, R.S.M., of Trinity College (Burlington), Secretary; and Prof. Thomas Ryan of St. Joseph's College (Philadelphia), Treasurer. In particular, the editor would like to thank the members of the Society's editorial board upon whose perceptive evaluation he has heavily relied: Rev. William Cenkner, O.P., of The Catholic University of America, and Rev. Thomas L. Sheridan, S.J., of St. Peter's College. Gratitude is also due to Prof. George Devine of Seton Hall University; Prof. Rodger Van Allen of Villanova University, who served as the local program chairman for the 1973 convention; Rev. Joseph A. Burke, S.J.; and to my colleagues in the theology department at Saint Joseph's College for their encouragement and support.

The editor also finds it a great pleasure to be able to express his gratitude to his wife, Monica, whose love and assistance have been beyond measure.

Thomas M. McFadden

Contents

III *Jesus and Contemporary Man*

PART I

CHRISTIAN DIVERSITY IN THINKING OF JESUS

The Challenge of Recent Research on the Gospels

JOSEPH A. GRASSI

Our principal source of information about Jesus has always been the four gospels. For many years we have been aware that these sources must be carefully sifted if we are to find detailed information about the earthly Jesus. The Gospels are confessional documents that are the final result of many years of teaching, preaching, instruction, and reflection by the Church on the life of Jesus. They are the view of a community that has looked back on Jesus' earthly career and understood it in terms of his resurrection and its own experience of the Holy Spirit. They are not first generation documents, but second generation reflections of the Church upon its origins.

In recent years a new element has been added that has much bearing on any quest for the historical Jesus. Recent research[1] on the Gospels has shown that these documents were written precisely to counter divergent views of Christian teachers (and their followers) who based their own quite unique life-styles on different views of Jesus himself. Previously we had known very little about these divergent, or so-called "false teachers." The gospel writers give only indirect references to them, and we have to read between the lines to get a sympathetic picture of these "other Christians" about whom they are speaking.

These divergent Christians were not considered as "heretics" in the early New Testament documents. They were regarded as brother Christians in communion with the rest of the community although they had decidedly different life-styles than other Christians. For the most part, the earlier New Testament documents were alarmed by tendencies in these groups, but had not yet condemned them.

Now, however, we have much new information to help us better understand the diversity in early Christianity. Among these are the findings at Nag Hammadi in Egypt in 1947, which are still being analyzed and interpreted by scholars. These manuscripts were part of a large gnostic Christian library.[2] Some of the best known include the gospel of Truth, the gospel of Thomas, and the gospel of Philip. The manuscripts, though written in Coptic around the fourth century A.D. are translations from much earlier Greek manuscripts. They contain sayings and parables of Jesus, a number of which are not in the New Testament. Even when they are found in the gospels, they are often related with a new gnostic twist. These new findings have greatly enriched our knowledge of early gnostic Christianity. Previously, we had depended on what we knew of a much more highly developed gnosticism of the second and third centuries, and even then we had to rely largely on second hand references of the early church Fathers[3] who certainly did not look upon the Gnostics with favor. Now, however, we have a clearer and much earlier picture that sheds light on many pages of the New Testament.

The collections of sayings and parables of Jesus in these documents may go back to traditions that even predate the canonical gospels. In fact, gnosticism may already have influenced many Jews before the time of Jesus and have entered the Church through Judaism.[4] Because of this new progress in biblical studies, we can find out a great deal more about the outlook of people whom we might call the "underground Christians" of the early Church. This will help us obtain a new appreciation of the unusual diversity that existed in early Christianity. Within the limitations of this essay, we can only sketch some of the results of this recent work on our understanding of the Gospels of Mark and Luke.

THE GOSPEL OF MARK

The key to understanding Mark is found in his chapter 13. For many Christians the events of the Jewish war with Rome, 66–70 A.D., were a decisive intervention of God that signaled the beginning of the last days of history and the imminent return of Jesus in glory. As a result, many Christians were looking for signs of this powerful coming. Some were claiming that Christ was already present in them and working in power: "Many will come in my name, saying, 'I am he'" (13:6). As a proof, they pointed to the miraculous signs and wonders they were able to produce. Mark has Jesus refer to them as "false Christs and false prophets" (13:21–22).

To confirm their views, these Christians appealed to a tradition about Jesus as a charismatic wonder-worker. This image was influenced by Jewish and Hellenistic views of the "charismatic figure as wonder-worker."[5] For example, Philo in his life of Moses portrays him as a great wise man

and worker of miracles.[6] He even calls Moses a *theios anēr,*
a divine man, and goes as far as naming him *theos,* a god,
when he writes, "this man is a god because he is wise."
Josephus is also familiar with this tradition. He writes of
false prophets who promised great wonders to the people
(*Antiquitates Judaicae* xx, v, 1). Especially noteworthy is
his mention of false prophets at the time of the fall of
Jerusalem who promised signs from heaven (*Bellum
Judaicum* vi, v, 2). This is an interesting link with Mark
in his concern over false Christs and prophets in connection with the Jerusalem tragedy (13:5 ff., 21–22).

To counter these views, one of Mark's principal methods
is to present the disciples and Peter as representative
figures.[7] They themselves had misunderstood Jesus in
terms of a "son of God" in the Hellenistic sense of a
wonder-worker, but had finally become "converted" to
knowing him as a Son of Man[8] who in his human condition,
through love, suffering, and finally death revealed himself
to be a powerful Son of God in an entirely new sense. In
part I of Mark, chapters 1 to 8:29, both the crowds and
disciples misunderstand Jesus' work in terms of a *theios
anēr,* a divine man characterized by miraculous signs and
wonders. Jesus himself appears dismayed by this understanding and often enjoins secrecy about his miracles. Even
when Peter confesses him to be Messiah (8:29), Jesus not
only enjoins him to silence (8:30), but even rebukes him.
This is because Peter's idea of the Messiah is wrong and
incomplete without an understanding that he is the Son
of Man who must first suffer, die, and rise again (8:31–33).

Since the disciples and Peter in the Gospel of Mark are
representative figures, we can piece together some general
characteristics of the type of Christian they represented in

Mark's church and the view of Jesus that they cherished. These Christians felt a tremendous divine power within them, perhaps that of Christ himself (13:6). This would manifest itself in external miraculous deeds of power (13:22). They would point to the stories of Jesus' exorcisms, healings, and miracles as an example to follow. The picture of Jesus in Mark's miracle source was most precious for them. At the height of the miracle collection was the multiplication of the loaves in Mark (6:30–46 and 8:1–10), a miracle with evident Eucharistic overtones in its resemblances to the Last Supper tradition. Probably Mark's opponents looked upon the Eucharist only in terms of the glorious presence of the *theios anēr* at a common meal that would revitalize their feelings of power. The misunderstanding of the loaves in Mark hints at this (8:14–21). Mark appears to have deliberately placed the Last Supper in the passion account although it probably had its origin as a separate story. In doing so, Mark plays down the original presentation of the Eucharist in his miracle collection source and re-presents it in terms of the passion and death of Jesus to emphasize the theme of the suffering Son of Man, and association with him in the breaking of the bread.[9]

There are some indications that Mark's opponents had a special regard for inner illumination, visions, and spiritual experiences since, strangely enough, Mark has no account of the post-resurrection appearances of Jesus (if we consider Mk. 16:8 as the original ending of the gospel according to a number of important Greek manuscripts). Why would Mark omit something that Paul considered a part of early Christian tradition as he enumerates the first apparitions of Jesus in 1 Cor. 15:1–9? It has been suggested that Mark has deliberately moved them from their original place after the resurrection to the earthly life of Jesus because his opponents appealed so much to their own visions and revelations of the risen Christ. Mark has probably moved [10] the essential resurrection appearance to his transfiguration story in 9:1–9. Here we have a vision of Jesus in glory that appears unlikely to have occurred in his early life. Another indication that Mark's opponents considered themselves as privileged by special secrets is found in Mark's treatment of Jesus' revelations to his disciples. Mark likes to show carefully that Jesus explains all things to his disciples: There are no special secrets guarded by a few chosen ones.

It appears then that Mark is deliberately modifying an image of Christ that appears in the miracle source collection in his Gospel. This would have been an earlier picture of Jesus as a charismatic wonder-worker who conveys this power to his disciples also. Like Jesus, some Christians trusted in the divine power within them, and prized their ability to come in immediate contact with God. In fact, some directly identified themselves with Jesus himself (13:6).

THE GOSPEL OF LUKE

There are special features of Luke's Gospel that can be best understood under the hypothesis that he is trying to counteract the influence of gnostic-oriented Christians in his audience. First let us give a brief sketch of what we mean by "gnostic-oriented" Christians in the first century. If we put together information from our sources, it is possible to sketch a picture of early gnosticism and its unique world view. As we do so, it must be kept in mind that there was no such thing as a universal gnostic "church." There were many distinct gnostic systems. In addition, each community had its own peculiar adaptation of gnostic ideas.

The word "gnosis" means nothing more than "knowledge." This knowledge centers on the basic conviction that each man has a piece of the divine, the *pneuma* locked within him. This is unrecognized by the world which is in "ignorance" of its true self. Thus men need to be awakened to know who they truly are and be able to tap this powerful presence within them. This can only come about through a special kind of inner illumination or gnosis. In later gnostic systems, the intellectual nature of this gnosis was greatly developed. However, it is likely that this is a corruption of an earlier, much more mystical gnosis. I say this because as time goes on, religions tend to lose their original charisma and become analytical systems. This is especially true when they are described in writing. In addition, there are many hints in the documents themselves that the "real thing" was an incommunicable secret revealed only to the "perfect." Hans Jonas has pointed out that the gospel of Truth describes a type of "gnosis" that is metaphysical and transforms both the individual and the universe.[11] So the gnosis or truth was probably some inner illuminatory, transforming experience of the hidden divine within man.

Gnosticism can be understood only in terms of the world view it embraces. Originally, there was only the one Light or God, and it was through some kind of emanation of this Light (a primal man in some myths) that the world came into existence. However, in this process, the emanated Light or primal man became divided up, scattered and im-

prisoned in human bodies. This was through the activity
of a hostile creator and other evil spirits who originally
came from the Light but somehow became separated from
it. The world and the material universe were held captive
by these spirits. The human body itself was under their
control and served as a trap or prison for the divine sparks
within that had originally come from the Light.

However, the Light never abandoned interest in the "lost
sheep," the scattered particles of divine Light or *Pneuma*.
It sent a redeemer or intermediary to liberate them. He did
not come in human flesh, for then he would also have
been in bondage and unable to help man. He came dis-
guised as a human being and thus was able to deceive the
evil spirits. The task of the messenger was to help men
find out who they truly were and teach them how to overcome the hostile cosmic powers and rejoin the true Light.

Through this redeemer, human beings would be led to
discover their true origin and obtain "salvation." This salvation was effected through an inner experience of the divine
spark within them. It was also accompanied by the "know-
how" to break the power of the evil cosmic spirits and the
world that kept them in bondage. Once they had learned to
escape, they could have freedom and immortality and
finally be able to rejoin the Light.

This new "freedom" had a profound effect on the life-
style of these pneumatics. They were a contemplative
group with a special esteem for inner mystical experiences.
There they really experienced "who they were." They also
had a new powerful confidence, or even boldness, for they
felt that they themselves were part of the divine. In addition they were supremely free and nonconformist; no
power on earth could hold them any longer.

As a result, they mistrusted the hostile world around them, which they regarded as a trap. The body itself, in their view, was a corruptible part of an evil universe. This made them deprecate the importance of the human body and sensual, especially sexual pleasures. On one side, some embraced a rigid asceticism, denying themselves the use of sex, marriage, and certain foods. On the other side, others felt that sex and other bodily pleasures could no longer really affect or touch them. Hence they could be supremely "free" of responsibility in the area of sexual contacts with others. After all, they were completely "above" the things of the body. Irenaeus complains of the libertinism of the second group, and also describes the rigid asceticism of the Encratites, who represented the first tendency (*Adversus Haereses* I, vi, 3; xxviii, 1).

In general, the Gnostics were a peace-loving group that kept to themselves. They had great esteem for their own community life, since it was there that the divine sparks could come together in anticipation of their final union. In these groups much of the pneumatic activity took place. As members "left" the body to enjoy their true selves in ecstasy, various types of psychic phenomena would result. This experience of the *pneuma* would become contagious, and a wave of excitement would sweep through the assembly. Irenaeus writes that Gnostics were accustomed to prophesy after reaching a "pitch of excitement" (*Adversus Haereses* I, xiii, 2).

They also felt a strong missionary responsibility. Men needed to be awakened from "sleep," aroused from their "drunkenness" so they could know the true light within them and escape the evil powers. Not to find the light would be to remain in everlasting ignorance which would finally result in being lost and destroyed with the world. Gnostic propaganda must have been quite widespread and effective to prompt such time-consuming efforts on the part of early church fathers to counteract their teachings.

It is easy to see how Christian converts of gnostic background could easily assimilate or even syncretize the teaching about Christ into their previous thought patterns. Christ could be understood as the divine intermediary from the true Light, who taught men to find the divine within them and to liberate them from the powers of the world. With their emphasis on the present, existential experience of the divine, it was easy for them to believe that there was no real coming end of history; the future was now in the present moment. As Christians, they tended to believe that the resurrection and ascension of Christ were the culmination of the end-period, and that through baptism they were able to enter into this final time. Some sayings of Jesus in the gnostic gospels appear to confirm this. The gospel of Thomas, saying 51, reads,

On what day will the rest for the dead come, and on what day will the new world come? He said to them, "That for which you are waiting has come but you do not recognize it."

The gospel of Philip, saying 90, reads,

Those who say, "A person will first die and then he will rise are in error." If one does not first receive the resurrection while still alive, one will receive nothing when he dies.

Luke takes special pains to counteract these views. To show that the ascension of Jesus is not an end point, he establishes a very definite time pattern of history in the first chapter of Acts.[12] He starts by speaking of all Jesus has done until the time of ascension. He then recalls the specific question of the disciples before this happened. They asked him, "Lord, will you at this time restore the kingdom to Israel?" (1:6). Jesus answers, "It is not for you to know the time which the Father has fixed by his own authority." They are then told by Jesus that they will receive the power of the Holy Spirit and become his witnesses in Jerusalem, Judea, Samaria, and even the ends of the earth. In other words, the Ascension is not the end-time of history. It will be followed by the gift of the Holy Spirit and a time span that will allow the gospel to be carried to the whole world.

According to Luke, it is only after this definite period of time that the return of Jesus and the new era will begin. Our author carefully brings this out in his record of the words of the two men dressed in white robes who witness the ascension, along with Jesus' disciples. The men say to them,

Men of Galilee, why do you stand here looking into the skies? This Jesus who was taken up from you into heaven will come in the same way that you saw him go into heaven (Acts 1:11).

In other words, the disciples are not to consider the ascension of Jesus as a stop-point to be "looked at" or contemplated, but as the sign of the beginning of an active mission to the world that must occur before the return of Jesus.

To drive home his conviction that there must be an interval of time for a world apostolate, Luke's Gospel from beginning to end is permeated with a strong atmosphere of universality. When the child Jesus is presented in the Temple, Simeon proclaims that the child is destined to be a "light of revelation to the Gentiles, and a glory for your people Israel" (2:32). Only Luke traces back the genealogy of Jesus to Adam, the father of the human race (3:38). In this universal theme, the Samaritans, who were not regarded as real Jews, receive special attention in the parable of the Good Samaritan and the account of the cure of the ten lepers, one of whom is a "foreigner" (10:29–37; 17:11–19). Corresponding to the mission of the twelve to Jewish towns, there is a mission (only in Luke) of Jesus' 72 disciples that is described in terms of a gentile apostolate—at least the direction not to be concerned about food observances hints at this (10:1–12).[13]

The last words of the risen Jesus in Luke's Gospel sum up this world-wide view. Jesus tells his disciples that repentance and forgiveness of sins should be preached to all nations beginning with Jerusalem (24:47). The Acts of the Apostles is written to show how the injunction of Jesus is carried out in action: first in Jerusalem, then in Judea, then in Samaria, and finally in the gentile world. The book ends on the triumphant note of the open preaching of the gospel by Paul at Rome, the center of the world.

The next critical concern of Luke is his opponents' view of Jesus' earthly life. The hardest reality for a gnostic-oriented Christian to accept was the full humanity of Jesus. As we have seen, the real thing for them was the divine spark within each man that was imprisoned by the hostile and evil matter in the universe. Enlightenment or *gnosis* meant a full escape from the power of the material world and a direct route to immortality. The reality of the suffering and death of Jesus was an almost impossible stumbling block for them. To avoid this dilemma, we do know from Irenaeus that some Christians believed that the divine Spirit came upon Jesus at his baptism and departed before his crucifixion and death (*Adversus Haereses* I, vii, 2). Some even claimed that Simon of Cyrene carried Jesus' cross and died in his stead. In the eyes of these Christians, Jesus was the divine stranger who took on only the appearance of human flesh in order to come into this world and enlighten men about their true origin.

Luke appears to be directly opposing this type of thinking about Jesus. He carefully teaches that Jesus was filled with the Holy Spirit from his mother's womb. The Holy Spirit came over Mary at the conception of Jesus, just as the presence of God overshadowed the desert meeting tent of Moses and came to dwell with the Hebrew people (Lk. 1:35; Ex. 40:34–38). In contrast, like any man, Jesus is circumcised on the eighth day, according to the Law. The baptism of Jesus, in comparison with Matthew, Mark, and John, appears to be de-emphasized in Luke. The coming of the Spirit seems more a result of Jesus' prayer than an effect of his actual baptism (3:21–22). This may be Luke's attempt to place his baptism in proper perspective as a stage in Jesus' life, rather than a dramatic beginning.

When it comes to describing Jesus' suffering and death, Luke adds further details to confirm that it was truly Jesus who died and no one else. In the story of Simon of Cyrene, he alone notes that Simon carried the cross *behind Jesus* (23:26; cf. Mk. 15:21; Mt. 27:32). To further identify Jesus as the same person on the cross, Luke relates how Jesus continued to speak to God as his father. In Mark and Matthew, Jesus' last cry appears to be wordless, but Luke interprets this in the words, "Father, into your hands I commend my spirit" (cf. Mk. 15:37; Mt. 27:50; and Lk. 23:34, according to many manuscripts).

In respect to the resurrection appearances of Jesus, gnostic Christians would be inclined to think of them essentially in terms of an inner divine illumination. To correct this, only in Luke do we find unusual efforts to present Jesus' resurrection in strictly physical and material terms, more like a resuscitation of his previous earthly life. Luke alone posits a period of forty days between Jesus' death and ascension, during which time he appears to his disciples and speaks to them on various occasions (Acts 1:3). In Luke, this interim period serves a special function as a time in which Jesus can *prove* himself truly alive (Acts 1:3).

In Luke alone (but cf. Jn. 20:26–29), the disciples receive concrete, tangible proofs that Jesus is alive. The appearance of Jesus is not enough for the incredulous disciples, so he actually eats some cooked fish in their presence (23:42). The Acts of the Apostles confirms this type of apologetic. Peter tells Cornelius that Jesus actually ate and drank with them after his resurrection (10:41). In this unusual type of presentation, Luke may be trying to answer the arguments of some Christians who claimed that divine messengers do not really eat and drink. They would cite the story of Tobit, where the angel Gabriel said that he did not really eat and drink but only appeared to do so (Tob. 12:19). In addition, only Luke specifically mentions that the women went to the tomb of Jesus and *did not find the body* (24:3). For Luke, apparitions are not enough, it must be the full human and tangible body of Jesus that rose from the dead.

CONCLUSION

We have seen that both Mark and Luke are dealing with the problem of earlier Christian diversity, and even images of Jesus that they are trying to normalize and correct. In the case of Mark it is the image of a powerful charismatic healer. In the case of Luke, if we read between the lines, it is the image of Jesus as a wisdom teacher who is enlightening men to find the divine within them here and now, rather than waiting for a future moment of history. Jesus becomes a model of a man who has himself experienced this enlightenment.

The results of this new approach to the Gospels help us to understand that the early Church did not move from unity to diversity, but from an early diversity to a gradual unity and conformity.[14] In other words, diversity was a spice of early Christianity, not a poison. This is an important reminder for the ecumenical movement of today. The emphasis should be on unity *in* diversity, recognizing, appreciating, and developing the special gifts in various Christian communities and churches, rather than an attempt to reduce them to a unity that stresses conformity. In addition, the gnostic-oriented Christians treasured the model of Jesus as the wisdom teacher directing men to find the divine within them. This Eastern influence can be an important ecumenical link between Western and Eastern religions, for it has been the latter that have continually drawn our attention to the inner divine element of man.

NOTES

[1] The work of Walter Bauer was a landmark of progress in this direction: *Orthodoxy and Heresy in Earliest Christianity,* eds. Robert A. Kraft and Gerhard Krodel (Philadelphia: Fortress, 1971). Since Bauer's original work in German which appeared in 1934, his essential thesis has been vindicated by recent scholarship. A critique of Bauer's work as well as an excellent summary of present directions in biblical research may be found in J.M. Robinson and Helmut Koester, *Trajectories Through Early Christianity* (Philadelphia: Fortress, 1971).

[2] For a complete listing as of 1968, see J. M. Robinson, "The Coptic Gnostic Library Today," *New Testament Studies* 14 (1968), pp. 356–401.

[3] Principal among these are the letters of Ignatius of Antioch, the works of Irenaeus of Lyons, especially his *Adversus Haereses,* and the works of Justin Martyr. All of these men wrote in the second century.

[4] See Robinson, *op. cit.,* pp. 66–67, where he points to the existence of apparently non-Christian Jewish gnosticism in texts found at Nag Hammadi.

[5] For an excellent study of this important background, see David Lenz Tiede, *The Charismatic Figure as Miracle Worker* (Society of Biblical Literature, Dissertation Series, Number One, 1972).

[6] Quotations from Philo are taken from Tiede's dissertation, p. 121.

[7] The insight that Peter and the disciples are representative figures for people of Mark's own time comes from T. J. Weeden, *Mark—Traditions in Conflict* (Philadelphia: Fortress, 1971).

[8] The understanding of the development of the Son of Man Christology as a response to a Greek "son of God" wonder-worker Christology is brought out by Norman Perrin in *Christology and a Modern Pilgrimage: A Discussion with Norman Perrin,* ed. Hans Betz (Claremont: New Testament Colloquium, 1971).

[9] Paul J. Achtemeier, "The Origin and Function of the Pre-Marcan Miracle Catenae," *Journal of Biblical Literature,* 91 (1972) 198–221.

[10] Suggested by Weeden, *op. cit.,* pp. 118–124.

[11] Hans Jonas, *The Gnostic Religion* (Boston: Beacon Press, 1963), pp. 309–319.

[12] For this understanding I am indebted to C. H. Talbert for his chapter, "The Redaction Critical Quest for Luke the Theologian," in *Jesus and Man's Hope* (Pittsburgh: Perspective, 1970).

[13] This mission of the 72 disciples is found only in the Gospel of Luke. The directive not to be concerned about food (10:8) would be especially important for a gentile apostolate. The preaching of the Kingdom of God

coming near (10:9) would also fit a gentile mission because for him this apostolate occurs just before the end time. In addition, the sending of the 72 parallels the choosing of the seven "deacons" in Acts 6:1-6, who are the ones who actually bring the Gospel to the non-Jewish world.

[14] This point has been developed by Robert L. Wilken, *The Myth of Christian Beginnings: History's Impact on Belief* (Garden City: Doubleday, 1971).

Mythological and Ontological Elements in Early Christology

SEELY BEGGIANI

Christianity, differing from primitive religions, presents itself as centered on an historical figure who was the vehicle of God's revelation and salvation. It sees in the historical life of Jesus and in the teaching and example arising from that life the authentic interpretation of how man should view God, the world, and himself. Stressing the disclosure of God in historical events, as seen in both the Old and New Testaments, it implies a rejection of the cyclical view of time and adopts what might be called a linear view of history culminating in an eschatological future.

It is the position of this article that Christian theology today (and, in fact, beginning at an early date) does not interpret Jesus entirely as a figure within linear history or as the historical Jesus saw himself. Because the meaning and the work of Christ went beyond human dimensions, he had to be grasped in mythological terms. While this was a necessary operation, there resulted a steady shift of emphasis from the earthly life of Jesus, to the Son of Man of the Parousia, to the Lord already reigning in the interim, to the pre-existent Logos and Son of God who descends and ascends. While the New Testament, for the most part, was concerned with the functional role of Jesus, the functional implied the ontic reality of Jesus and the ontic was eventually to lead to the ontological. By the fifth century the Son of God of the Scriptures had become God the Son, and the historical Jesus had become the incarnation of a divine person of the same substance with two other divine persons. Meanwhile, the eschatological "end of days" of the Old Testament had given way to the beginning of the end of days in the Resurrection. But, with the delay of the end of the end of days, the Parousia was first de-emphasized and then discarded. With the influence of Greek philosophy we have a dualism both of body and soul, and of spiritual and material worlds. Emphasis now rests on the immorality of the individual soul and its escape from linear history.[1]

The concern of this paper is that not only was Christ mythologized, and the mythology ontologized, but that the tendency among many Christians today is to take both the mythological and ontological interpretations literally. Secondly, while on the one hand many Christians speak of salvation history and therefore of linear history, on the other hand they speak of mystically grafting themselves onto the heavenly New Adam and view the death and resurrection of Christ as archetypal of the destiny of the individual soul.

Before proceeding, we should make two clarifications: first, what do we mean by taking symbols literally, and secondly, is the purpose of this paper merely to come to the defense of the principle of analogy. Regarding the first point, Ricoeur explains that symbol conceals a double intentionality. The first intentionality is the literal meaning of the symbol, but the literal and manifest sense points beyond itself to a second intentionality. However, differing from "transparent and technical signs, which say what they want to say in positing that which they signify, symbolic signs are opaque, because the literal, obvious meaning itself points analogically to a second meaning which is not given otherwise than in (the symbol)." The analogical relation that connects the second meaning with the first cannot be objectified. "It is by living in the first meaning that I am led by it beyond itself; the symbolic meaning is constituted in and by the literal meaning which effects the analogy in giving the analogue." It is unlike a comparison from the outside, because in the symbol the primary meaning "makes us participate in the latent meaning and thus assimilates us to that which is symbolized without our being able to master the similitude intellectually." [2] Symbols are taken literally when the first intentionality is taken as the reality itself. Fawcett, speaking of metaphors, comments that the history of the doctrine of the atonement bears witness to the danger that was present in the use of such metaphorical expressions as "a ransom for many," "lamb without blemish," or "our great high priest." [3]

Regarding the second point, while we are concerned with the proper understanding of analogy, this article is not directed toward analogy as it is used in philosophy which relies exclusively on reason and attempts to handle the transcendent within the categories of objective and abstract thinking. Rather, we wish to give full meaning to the analogical character of symbol as it is found embedded in symbols and myths. Symbols appeal primarily to the imagination. The analogy within any symbol cannot be "isolated from it and handled as though it were part of a propositional argument. Symbolic language severely limits the analogical element, qualifying it and shaping it in order that it should not be used discursively." [4]

It is the purpose of this paper to study the mythological interpretation given Jesus in early Christology by analyzing such titles as Son of Man, Lord, Wisdom-Logos, Son of God, and New Man. The issue is not to speculate on whether these titles were borrowed or derived from Babylonian, Greek, or gnostic myths. We grant that Christians developed a mythological framework, which was peculiar to them especially in being centered on an historical individual. Nevertheless, their interpretive method was analogous to the dynamics of interpretation operative in all religions. Some examples will be given of how these symbols were later philosophized. An attempt will be made to show how eschatology was reinterpreted and attention focused on the destiny of the individual soul. Finally, we shall conclude by stressing that what is called for is an admission of the hermeneutical presuppositions and problems, and an attempt to search for the meaning contained in the myth and the ontology.

CHRISTOLOGY IN THE EARLY CHURCH

The task of the early Church was to interpret and assess the meaning and the work of Jesus. As we have indicated, it had to rely on the language of its own religious consciousness, especially the language of Jewish messianism and eschatology. It undertook the work of reinterpretation and re-mythologization. We shall limit our analysis to the more significant and provocative titles attributed to Jesus, and begin with a few observations regarding the title Son of Man.

Son of Man

Jesus had claimed that his message and offer of salvation would be vindicated at the "end" by the Son of Man. But the early Church declared that it is Jesus himself who will return as the triumphant Son of Man very shortly. According to Fuller:

By identifying Jesus in his earthly life with the coming Son of Man the early Church was making an affirmation about the authority of the earthly Jesus in his word and work . . . the "most primitive Christology of all" revolves around two poles, the earthly work of Jesus as proleptic Son of Man and his future coming in glory as the transcendent Son of Man . . . [Jesus] had truly brought, as he had claimed, the final eschatological word and deed of God.[5]

Therefore, it was the Son of Man motif that allowed the Palestinian church to connect Jesus' second coming with his first.

To appreciate the mythological characteristics of this title, it is helpful to note its origins. Some have seen its origin in the oriental gnostic myth of the Heavenly Man, while others look to the Old Testament Jewish tradition itself. Feuillet is cited as believing it to be a combination of the prophetic Messiah, the Ezechielic Son of Man as title for the prophet, and the hypostatization of Wisdom in sapiential literature. Fuller concludes that while the problem of origin is unsolved, he would look for its roots in Jewish prophetic expectation. "But just as under foreign

(Persian) influence the prophetic eschatology was transcendentalized in apocalyptic, so too it is reasonable to suppose that it was under the same foreign influence that the agent of redemption was transcendentalized into the Son of Man." [6] In Ethiopian Enoch, his pre-existence is declared and he has characteristics of both Royal messianism and the servant of Yahweh in Isaiah. He lives in heaven from the beginning of time until he comes to earth at the end of time.[7] Schnackenburg adds that the Johannine Son of Man is connected with Wisdom speculation. As in Wisdom literature, the Son of Man appears on earth (Bar. 3:37 ff.) and reveals heavenly things (Wis. 9:16 ff.); he moves between heaven and earth, the realm "above" and the realm "below" (Bar. 3:29) and brings men divine revelation for their salvation.[8]

The point we wish to make is that with the title Son of Man, the historical Jesus is already interpreted as a transcendental figure and cosmic judge. There are intimations of pre-existence, and while we cannot say that he is compared with primeval man, it will not be long before Paul will conceive of Christ as Second Adam, the man from heaven, the uncorrupted "image of God."

Lord

With the postponement of the Parousia, attention focused on the work of Jesus as being evaluated for its own sake. Furthermore, exaltation Christology grew out of the deepening of present experience, particularly of the Holy Spirit, in the continuing life of the Church. It was perceived that Jesus rules as the present Lord over his Church, over the life of each individual. According to Cullmann, this new understanding was given to the first Christians in common worship, above all in the common meals, and confirmed in the various expressions of their life together. The connection between the present Lord and the earthly Jesus was understood on the basis of Psalm 110 to which Jesus himself had already referred as the "exaltation" of the risen Christ "to the right hand of God." Therefore in Acts 2:36, in view of the above psalm, Jesus becomes Lord and Christ from the moment of his ascension and is henceforth actively reigning.[9]

Tentative beginnings are made in transferring to Jesus the Septuagint passages referring to Yahweh-Lord. For example, Paul describes the second coming as "the day of Christ" or "the day of our Lord Jesus Christ" or "the day of the Lord" reflecting a non-literal interpretation of the "day of the Lord" of the Old Testament. Paul's statement that Jesus will come "with all his saints" reflects an interpretation of the Old Testament that "the Lord my God shall come and all the saints with him (Zech. 14:5). Paul's conviction that "then shall the wicked be revealed, whom the Lord shall destroy with the breath of his mouth" reflects again an interpretation of the Old Testament concerning "the rod out of the stem of Jesse" that "with the breath of his lips shall destroy the wicked" (Is. 11:4).[10]

However, at this stage, all that is involved is a transference of functions from God to the exalted Jesus. Or rather, it is precisely through the exalted Jesus that God carries out these functions.[11] According to the early Christian faith, this Lord is of course also pre-existent. If Christ is one with God in his resurrection, he must have been united with God from the beginning.[12]

Wisdom-Logos

We first meet Logos and Wisdom in really hypostatic form in an Alexandrian environment, in Hellenistic Judaism. According to Cullmann we must reckon with extra-Jewish influences of a mediator figure of pagan mythology. As a result of Platonic and partly perhaps mythological influences, Philo too prepares the way for the conception of a personified mediator. Also, rabbinical texts identify pre-existent wisdom with the Torah.[13] For Paul, the pre-existent wisdom or law is the pre-existent Messiah. The revelation of the Law of Moses and the birth of Jesus are to him two successive stages in the earthly revelations of pre-existent wisdom. He also applies to the Messiah the terms by which pre-existent wisdom was traditionally described.[14] Therefore, the term "wisdom" offered the possibility of an interpretation of Christ as the pre-existent agent of creation and the government of the world, and as the agent of revelation of religious truth. It also ultimately offered the possibility of interpreting the historical emergence of Jesus in terms of a descent from heaven, and this would certainly affect the developing doctrine of the Incarnation.

In reference to the expression "Logos (Word) of God," there are many passages in the Old Testament in which, following the first chapter of Genesis, the Word of God is made the object of independent consideration because of its powerful effect, even though it may not yet be personified. When one reflects on the Creation, the idea comes that every creative self-revelation of God to the world happens through his word.

Also, we should remember that the Logos doctrine of
Philo was intended to bridge the gulf between the purely
spiritual God and the material world, and also to explain
the presence and action of God in the soul. Like wisdom,
the Logos is distinct from, yet intimately related to, the
being of God, and like wisdom (Wis. 7:26), the Philonic
Logos is the image of God and the agent of revelation.
Philo identified divine wisdom as it appears in the later
books of the Old Testament with the Logos and hence
established the connection between the terms used in the
Jewish bible and that of Hellenistic philosophy.[15]

There are great similarities between Philo's understand-
ing and use of the term Logos and that of the Prologue of
John. Like Philo, who speaks of the pre-existent Logos as
that "through which the world was framed," and like the
Wisdom of Solomon which speaks of pre-existent wisdom
as "the artificer of all things," John says concerning the
Logos: "All things were made through him." Nevertheless,
John's use of the term rests on the close connection between the origin of all revelation and the historical life of
Jesus. The Johannine statements about the Logos are the
result of deep theological reflections about the life of Jesus
as the central revelation of God.[16] And, John's declaration
of the pre-existence of the Logos and his descent and as-
cent is an attempt to establish Christ's power to save.[17]

With the title, "Wisdom-Logos" the early Church was
in a position to speak not only of the pre-existence of Jesus,
but a pre-existent one who reveals through history. All
things were made through him, and he descends and ascends to God. The historical Jesus becomes but a small
segment in a line of history that has no beginning or end.

Son of God

We speculate that Jesus used the term "Abba" to indicate that he was conscious of a unique sonship to which he was able to admit others through his eschatological ministry. Fuller claims that Ps. 2:7 was first used by the Palestinian church to refer to the moment Jesus was predestined to exercise the office of eschatological judge at the Parousia.[18] With the shift of emphasis from the Parousia to the exaltation and present Lordship of Jesus, it was only natural that the term "Son of God" should be transferred to the exaltation. David's accession now typifies the enthronement of Jesus after his resurrection.

According to Cullmann, the Jewish concept of the Son of God is essentially characterized by the idea of election to participate in divine work through the execution of a particular commission. When Jesus speaks of himself in the Synoptics as Son of God or Son, it is to refer either to the obedience of the Son in fulfillment of the divine plan, or to the secret that he is aware that he is related to God as no other man is.[19]

In conformity with the then current view that it is the Messiah whom in Scripture God addresses as "my Son" and concerning whom he says, "Also I will make him my first-born," and taking the Messiah spoken of in these verses to refer to the pre-existent Messiah who was created before the creation of the world, Paul speaks of the pre-existent Christ as God's "own Son" or as "his Son," describing him also as "the first-born of all creation" and as one who was "before all things." [20]

Then, in the Christological hymn of Phil. 2:6–11, we see

a shift from the enthronization of Jesus to his exalted origin in a pre-existent state. The Incarnation is undertaken upon the redeemer's own pre-incarnate initiative. The idea of an interim of "already and not yet" with its struggles gives way to the claim that the enemies are all subjugated from the moment of the enthronization. According to Fuller, this hymn uses materials provided by the wisdom and anthropos myth already current in Hellenistic Judaism. Presupposed throughout this hymn is the Hellenistic worldview, with its three-storied universe consisting of heaven, earth, and underworld. In the final stanza the exalted one is identified as Lord, the Septuagint rendering of Yahweh. Henceforth God exercises his Lordship through the incarnate Son and obedient one who has been exalted.[21]

New Man

Perhaps it is Paul's concept of the New Man which shows best an analogy between the Christian understanding and mythological elements in other religions. Besides what we have said above of the title "Son of Man," consideration must be given to the development of the heavenly Man-image idea under the influence of passages from Genesis. In fact, in some Jewish-Hellenistic writings Adam is exalted to a heavenly position. Such writings as the Life of Adam and Eve, the Apocalypse of Moses, and the Testament of Abraham view him as a heavenly being.[22]

One fundamental difference between the Judeo-Christian teaching and that of others regarding the Primeval Man is that for the former, Adam, the first man, had sinned. According to Cullmann, the Pauline answer was to combine both the ideas of Servant of Yahweh and Son of Man. Therefore, the mission of the Heavenly Man was to redeem men by making them what he himself is, the image of God. Since the first man, Adam, the representative of all men, sinned, the Heavenly Man, the divine prototype of humanity, must therefore himself enter sinful humanity in order to free it from its sins. Paul's conclusion is that the "Man" who alone is and has retained the image of the creator can form us according to this image when we "put on the new man." [23]

Jesus is seen as the archetype of the primal man out of whose being all life came. Paul tells us that Jesus, as the source of life, is the body of which each Christian is the member. He is the head of the body and the New Adam. Ricoeur's interpretation of St. Paul arises out of his study of pardon. He claims that pardon as something experienced gets its meaning from the participation of the individual in the "type" of the fundamental man. Therefore, Paul's "putting on the new man" signifies symbolically a participation in the types of the first and second Adam. What gives ontological weight to these types in Paul is the faith that Jesus himself, a historical man, "exists in the form of God" and that he fulfills the type, the form, the image. "It is not that the individual undergoes a certain experience and then projects it into the world of images: on the contrary, it is because he is incorporated into that which those 'images' signify that the individual attains the experience of pardon." [24] Also, the remission of debt is the acquittal at the great trial in which the fundamental man is judge and advocate. Ricoeur sees not only a juridical symbol of acquittal but the mystical symbolism of the graft of life which manifests the intimate connection between the infusion of life and the gratuitousness of the grace of acquittal.[25]

While the Christian message, namely God's manifestation and salvation in Jesus, remains basically the same through this whole evolution, the Christology at the end of the New Testament era is quite changed from how Jesus saw himself. The Parousia becomes quite distant and greatly de-emphasized; the earthly work of Jesus now needs no vindication because he was the "image of God" and the "one through whom the world was created" from the beginning. Jesus' role is quite clear to him even before his conception because the Incarnation is taken on his initiative. The life and work of Jesus is only a brief segment in his eternal existence. The ascended Jesus now becomes not only Lord and Son of God, but the New Adam, the Primeval Man. The role of the Christian is not only to accept divine forgiveness and love, to work for the eschaton, and to realize the action of the exalted Christ on the Church living in the "already and not yet," but also to "put on the image" of the New Adam and to "graft oneself" onto the body of the Heavenly Man. Granted this is all symbolic interpretation, there is always the danger that it will be taken literally.

THE FATHERS AND ONTOLOGY

We have seen that the functional affirmations of earliest Christology gave way to ontic conclusions. Now in the era of the Fathers ontic assertions were to lead to ontological questions.

A good example of how the ontological development occurred is seen in the interpretation given to the term Logos. In the second and third centuries, it was transposed into philosophical and cosmological terms. Hellenistic theology presupposed that there must be a mediator between God, who is simple unity, unchangeable and perfect being, and the sphere of multiplicity, change, and temporality—that, indeed, there cannot be divine creation without a mediator. If God was present and active in Christ, involved in the world of time and space, this was not God the Father but the mediating Logos of God. Hence the great problem for patristic theology was the relation between the Logos and the Father: How far and in what sense the Logos mediates God to the world, to what degree does the Logos communicate the divine essence itself. Lampe claims that the Father addressed by Jesus as Abba had come to be identified with the Father of the universe in the *Timeas*, and the idea of the Logos, adopted to interpret the relation of Christ's Lordship to God and to the world, had been assimilated to the divine Mind of Neoplatonism.[26] Pelikan states that for some of the Fathers the Logos, through whom God made all things, was God's power and wisdom, and was the agent through whom God had dealt with mankind, achieving his purpose of creation and revealing his will. This very Logos, principle of creation and rationality of speech and revelation, had become incarnate.[27] The Logos, God's self-communication in creation, revelation, and salvation was Hellenized as the divine mediator coming from God and immanent in the cosmos.[28]

Many of the Fathers from Justin to Clement of Alexandria were influenced by the Philonic Logos. They seemed to have identified the Johannine Logos with the Philonic

Logos. Justin, for example, declares that "before the work of creation the Logos was with the Father and was begotten." [29] The doctrine of the *Logos spermatikos* is already taken up by Justin; the distinction between the *logos endiathetos* and the *logos prophorikos* appears in Theophilus of Antioch. An attempt was being made to provide a starting-point for a general understanding of reality, including man and his nature. Nothing of the sort can be found in the restricted perspective of John, which is entirely concentrated on Christ as the Logos.[30]

With the general acceptance of the miraculous birth of Jesus, the Christian God assumed the character of a begetter with regard to the earthly born Christ; he also became a begetter with regard to the pre-existent heavenly Christ. Origen's description of the generation of the Logos from God is expressed in the same terms as is found in Plotinus' description of the generation of the *nous* from the One. The Logos is thus no longer created; it was generated in the more literal sense of the term and it was called "son" and "first-born" and "only-begotten" also in a more literal sense of the terms.[31]

Therefore, we have a shift from the idea of an actually pre-existent Son of God to the very different theological concept of God the Son. The pre-existent Christ was no longer created by God after the analogy of the handiwork of an artisan; he was generated by God after the analogy of the offspring of a human father. Therefore, he was God like his Father, just as every human son generated by a human father is a man like his father. Philosophically minded church Fathers found support for this kind of reasoning in the philosophic principle that that which is generated must be of the same species as that which generates it. It was under this changed conception of the origin of the pre-existent Christ that Paul's declaration that Christ was "equal with God" and John's declaration that "the Logos was God" began to be taken literally. The pre-existent Christ, now identified with the Logos, was not merely divine, he was God.[32] Lampe adds that the designation "Son" involved a constant tendency to project on to the eternal Logos the attributes of human personality. The tendency was to think of the Son as a heavenly person on the analogy of a human person.[33]

In this partial presentation of the ontological interpretation given to the Christological symbols we see that Jesus is not only pre-existent but begotten of the Father and of one substance with the Father. He becomes the divine mediator bridging the transcendence of God and earth. Later on he is declared to be an incarnate divine person who united in himself two natures, divine and human. He is not only Son of God but God the Son, one person of a Trinity of persons.

The issue raised by this paper is whether by the time we have reached the ontological stage, we realize the distance we have put between ourselves and the historical Jesus of the Scriptures. While the Christological and philosophical interpretations might have been valid, there is the danger of their being taken literally and therefore becoming a possible obstacle to reaching Jesus.

ESCHATOLOGY RE-EVALUATED

Not only had changes in interpretation been taking place regarding the life and work of Christ, but the Judeo-Christian view of time and history underwent re-evaluation as Christology came more and more in contact with Greek philosophy. The Greek mentality stressed a more circular view of history. For it, redemption has as its goal to be freed from time itself. Redemption through divine action in the course of events in time is impossible. Redemption in Hellenism can consist only in the fact that we are transferred from existence in this world, an existence bound to the circular course of time, into that Beyond which is removed from time and is already and always available. From the Old Testament, Christian thought had learned to look upon time and history as the stage for God's activity. For the Christian, the coming consummation is an actual future in time, just as the past redemptive deed of Jesus Christ. The New Testament knows only the linear time concept of today, yesterday, and tomorrow; all philosophical reinterpretation and dissolution into timeless metaphysics is foreign to it.[34]

The collapse of the primitive Christian eschatological expectation hastened the adoption of the spatial metaphysical scheme of Hellenism. Also, as we have seen, some early Christian language about Christ does flirt with the possibility of describing the crucial points of his birth and death as mere dots in the circumference of a large circle.[35]

Clement of Alexandria is said to have understood by the Parousia not an event in the immediate future, but something that has already been fulfilled with the coming of Jesus as the Logos made flesh. Origen's teaching is said to be not a Platonized form of genuine Christian eschatology, but an alternative to or indeed an evasion of eschatology.[36]

When the apocalyptic vision was eclipsed, however,

many of the words and deeds in the Scriptures seemed enigmatic. Much Gospel interpretation during the second and third centuries consisted in the effort to make sense of apocalyptic passages when the presuppositions had shifted. On the other hand, partly because of the conservative influence of the creeds, eschatological language and apocalyptic imagery continued to occupy a prominent place in Christian speech even when the imminent return of Christ was not vividly expected as it once had been.[37]

Ever since the first Christian died, as the language of I Thessalonians chapter four shows, the end of history and the end of an individual life stand in significant but confusing relationship for Christian thought. As the expectation that history is about to end recedes in prominence, individual death takes over many of the functions previously assigned to this expectation in Christian hope and faith. Deliverance is an act of God's intervention, not the pinnacle of man's achievement.[38]

As we have implied above, under the influence of Origen and his disciples the universal history of the soul began to replace finality and particularity. Gregory of Nyssa developed the Origenist idea of the soul into a full-blown mysticism. In his book, *On the Soul and Resurrection,* we see strong indications that the immortality of the soul as presented in the *Phaedo* dominates the treatise and transmutes the finality of Christ and of the Resurrection into a mere corollary of a universal doctrine of immortality. The finality of the Last Judgment was universalized into a harmonization of all things with the Good.[39]

We had characterized the Judeo-Christian view of history as linear and eschatological. However, with the postpone-

ment of the Parousia, with questions arising concerning
the destiny of individual Christians who had died, and
with more and more contact with the world of Greek philosophy, conditions were set for a fusion of the Christian
mind with Neo-Platonic spirituality which Ricoeur describes as "the remote heir of the myth of the exiled soul
and the body person." [40] Along with the Greek dualism of
body and soul, there was the dualism of the earthly and
heavenly worlds, and a view of the universe as an eternally
static reality. Rather than being a matter of all men striv-
ing to achieve the consummation of the earth, salvation became a matter purely of the individual soul being delivered from the body up into the heavenly world. By seeing Jesus' life and death as archetype of the end, individual
man's own anxiety is put at rest. While not denying that
the New Testament message of God's salvation and redemption has been retained, we have come a long way
from the view of history found in the Scriptures.

IMPLICATIONS

Granted that Christology contains mythological interpretations of Jesus, one must distinguish between how
Jesus saw himself, how he appears in developed New
Testament Christology, and the ontological interpretation
of the Fathers. If Christology makes use of mythological
and ontological elements then we must be sure to understand the meaning contained in the myth and in the ontology, and beware not to take images and concepts
literally. After attempting to find the underlying meaning,

we must study how to convey it to man today and perhaps how to go about a relevant re-interpretation of myth.

For example, it would seem that Christology on the whole attempts through a wide range of concepts and images to convey God's "outreach" toward men, his self-disclosure, and the communication and imparting of himself to them.[41] It also strives to express the singularity of Jesus' relationship to God and his role as bearer of God's self-communication to the world. Such references as God's sending his Son into the world and the miraculous birth of Jesus are an attempt to emphasize that Jesus' history does not merely emerge out of the ongoing history of men, but is the direct, invasive act of God from outside all human possibilities.[42]

We can speculate that the meaning of the title "Lord" lies in the conviction that Jesus uniquely mediated God's authority and that he transcended the category of ordinary humanity. On the other hand, the idea of Logos attempts to express the incarnation of God's creative self-utterance, the embodiment of his self-communication to the world.[43]

The term "Son of God" has the idea of faithful adherence to the law amid persecution, and of final vindication by God. It could express that in Jesus the messianic expectations have been fufilled. Jesus in a far fuller sense than the Israelite king (Ps. 2:7) was God's elect agent and the focus of man's response of obedience toward God. Jesus conveys the revelatory presence and saving action of God himself.[44]

The basic thrust of Scripture is to declare that God is a God who goes out of himself and who was uniquely present in Jesus Christ. The early Christians and all succeeding generations have sought to express this divine intimacy in Christ and its meaning for man's redemption and salvation in the most adequate forms possible. The Christians of the first centuries succeeded by reconfiguring and re-interpreting the religious mythological frameworks and philosophical systems of their era. It is our task to seek out and try to grasp the meaning they sought to embody, and to re-formulate it for our time. In pursuing this work, we must re-examine critically those expressions which now may tend to obscure rather than bring to light the reality which is Christ.

NOTES

[1] A partial bibliography on these issues would include the works of Ricoeur, Fawcett, Fuller, Schnackenburg, Cullmann, Wolfson, Borsch, and Pelikan cited below. See also Friedrick Gogarten, *Christ the Crisis,* trans. R. A. Wilson (Richmond: John Knox Press, 1970); Van Harvey, *The Historian and the Believer* (New York: Macmillan, 1966); Joachim Jeremias, *New Testament Theology,* trans. J. Bowden (New York: Scribner, 1971); S. W. Sykes and J. P. Clayton, *Christ, Faith and History* (Cambridge: Cambridge Univ. Press, 1972).

[2] Paul Ricoeur, *The Symbolism of Evil,* trans. E. Buchanan (Boston: Beacon Press, 1967), pp. 14–16.

[3] T. Fawcett, *The Symbolic Language of Religion* (Minneapolis: Augsburg, 1971), p. 52.

[4] *Ibid.*, pp. 60–61.

[5] Reginald Fuller, *Foundations of New Testament Christology* (New York: Scribner, 1965), pp. 148–51.

[6] *Ibid.*, pp. 36 ff.

[7] While not attempting to indicate derivation there is an interesting parallel between the Jewish Son of Man and the Babylonian Son of Man. The latter was rooted in the more ancient myth of primordial man. Primordial man was divine by nature and the son of the most high God. He was created by the Lord so that he in turn would bring forth crea-

tion. He was the prototype of all righteous men, but also an eschatological figure who in the end of time would establish paradise for all men. He would be victorious over the forces of evil. Presently he was hidden within the most high God, but one day he would come on the clouds in glory to judge the living and the dead. On the other hand, the Greek god, Anthropos, also was a divine pre-existent being. He was a cosmic figure, the mystical expression of the world. He was the first man, the preacher of righteousness. He would redeem man from his material prison. He would be the redeemer and savior of all mankind and his spirit would dwell in those who would follow his ways. He would reveal himself to men by coming on the clouds in glory and he would bring resurrection to all men. On this point, cf. William Duggan, *Myth and Christian Belief* (Notre Dame, Indiana: Fides, 1971), pp. 110–111.

[8] Rudolf Schnackenburg, *The Gospel According to Saint John*, volume 1, trans. K. Smyth (New York: Herder and Herder, 1968), pp. 538–42.

[9] Oscar Cullmann, *Christology of the New Testament*, trans. S. Guthrie and C. Hall (Philadelphia: Westminster, 1959), p. 320.

[10] H. A. Wolfson, *The Philosophy of the Church Fathers,* volume 1, (Cambridge, Mass.: Harvard University Press, 1964), pp. 41–42.

[11] Fuller, *op. cit.,* pp. 184 ff.; Cullmann, *op. cit.,* p. 234.

[12] Cullmann, *op. cit.,* p. 235.

[13] *Ibid.,* pp. 255–57. In post-biblical Wisdom literature, the pre-existence of wisdom is expressed in such statements as that "before them all was wisdom created" (Sirach 1:4) and that before the creation of the world wisdom was the "only begotten" (Wis. 7:22) and of "noble birth" (Wis. 8:3). In rabbinical literature the Messiah and the Law are listed among the seven things which "were created before the creation of the world."

[14] Wolfson, *op. cit.,* pp. 156–60. We might add that drawing upon the description of wisdom in the Wisdom of Solomon as "a breath of the power of God," and "an image of his goodness," Paul describes the pre-existent Christ as "the power of God and the wisdom of God." Then like the pre-existent wisdom, which is described again in the Wisdom of Solomon as the "artificer of all things," the pre-existent Christ is described by Paul as he by whom "all things were created."

[15] Schnackenburg, *op. cit.,* p. 486. The Logos of Philo, as also the wisdom of the Wisdom of Solomon, is conceived to have three stages of existence, two before the creation of the world and one after its creation. First, it existed from eternity as a thought of God. Second, prior to the creation of the world it was created by God as a real incorporeal being and was used by God as an instrument or rather a plan in the creation of the world. Third, with the creation of the world, God implanted the

Logos and, as immanent, it acts as the instrument of divine providence. Wolfson, *op. cit.*, p. 177.

[16] Cullmann, *op. cit.*, pp. 262–64.

[17] Schnackenburg, *op. cit.*, pp. 555–56.

[18] Fuller, *op. cit.*, pp. 166–67.

[19] Cullmann, *op. cit.*, pp. 275–283.

[20] Wolfson, *op. cit.*, pp. 159 ff.

[21] Fuller, *op. cit.*, pp. 205–213.

[22] F. Borsch, *The Christian and the Gnostic Son of Man* (Naperville, Illinois: Allenson, 1970), pp. 117–118.

[23] Cullmann, *op. cit.*, pp. 172–174.

[24] Ricoeur, *op. cit.*, pp. 274–75.

[25] *Ibid.*, pp. 276–78.

[26] G. Lampe, "The Holy Spirit and the Person of Christ," in *Christ, Faith and History*, eds. S. W. Sykes and J. P. Clayton (Cambridge: Cambridge Univ. Press, 1972), pp. 114–15.

[27] Jaroslav Pelikan, *The Emergence of the Catholic Tradition (100–600)* (Chicago: University of Chicago Press, 1971), pp. 187–88.

[28] The Fathers adopted from Philo the belief that the Platonic ideas in their totality were contained in an incorporeal mind called Logos. But, the Fathers, in departure from Philo, made the Logos, even after it came to exist by the side of God, one with God, so that both of them form one simple and indivisible Godhead. Accordingly, the ideas contained in the Logos are said to be contained in the one simple and indivisible Godhead, and are no longer considered, as in Philo, as existing outside of God. Cf. Wolfson, *op. cit.*, p. 96.

[29] *Ibid.*, pp. 192 ff.

[30] Schnackenburg, *op. cit.*, pp. 482–83.

[31] When later the Philonic conception of the Logos as created out of nothing was revived by Arius, his view was anathematized as heresy. In the Creed of Nicaea it was formally declared that he was "begotten of the Father . . . ," that is, of the substance of the Father. Thus in Christianity, the Logos of Philo, when transferred to the pre-existent Christ ceased to be created by God and became begotten by God. Cf. Wolfson, *op. cit.*, pp. 202–292.

[32] *Ibid.*, p. 307.

[33] Lampe, *op. cit.*, p. 122.

[34] Oscar Cullmann, *Christ and Time*, trans. Floyd Filson (Philadelphia: Westminster, 1950), pp. 37–65.

[35] Jaroslav Pelikan, *The Shape of Death* (New York: Abingdon, 1961), pp. 48–50.

[36] Pelikan, *The Emergence of the Catholic Tradition* (*100–600*), p. 128.

[37] *Ibid.*, pp. 126–30.

[38] Pelikan, *The Shape of Death*, p. 67.

[39] Jaroslav Pelikan, *The Finality of Jesus Christ in an Age of Universal History* (Richmond: John Knox Press, 1965), pp. 19–21.

[40] Ricoeur, *op. cit.*, p. 335.

[41] Lampe, *op. cit.*, pp. 111–12.

[42] Fuller, *op. cit.*, p. 254.

[43] Lampe, *op. cit.*, pp. 111–14.

[44] Fuller, *op. cit.*, pp. 72, 228–29, 254–55; Lampe, *op. cit.*, p. 113.

Re-thinking the Relationship Between Jesus and the Old Testament

C. GILBERT ROMERO

Few problems have appeared so simple yet proven so complex as the question of Jesus and the Old Testament. The history of biblical studies has shown us various solutions, ranging from Marcion's denial of the Old Testament's validity to Wilhelm Vischer's seeing Jesus everywhere in its pages. Any solution between these extremes has to consider two factors in dealing with the problem, namely realization that the question is primarily a theological one, and an admission that the ultimate criterion for establishing a relationship between the Testaments will be a faith judgment. What is at issue is to consider whether the relationship between the Testaments is one of continuity or one of discontinuity. That is to say, does the interpreter begin from the Old Testament and work through to the New? Or does he begin from the New and work back into the Old?

With this in mind, we can critically examine proposed solutions which, for the sake of convenience, may be reduced to four: typology, *sensus plenior* or "fuller sense," Christocentrism, and promise and fulfillment.

Typology, as championed by Gerhard von Rad and others, sees a relationship of correspondence in persons, events, or institutions either in terms of similarity or of contrast.[1] The typological relationship is based on the power of the analogy that the God of Abraham, Isaac, and Jacob is the same God who is the Father of Jesus Christ. Von Rad is quick to point out that typology is not allegory because typology has a historical basis and is to be guided by the kerygma to prevent arbitrariness. One of the most cogent objections to be raised against typology is its inability to establish the criterion of validity and limitations outside of the interpretation itself. That is to say, typology seems to bring in meaning from *outside* the Old Testament.

The second proposed solution is that of the *sensus plenior* or "fuller sense," which is defined as "the deeper meaning, intended by God but not clearly intended by the author, as seen to exist in the words of Scripture when studied in the light of further revelation."[2] Thus understood, the *sensus plenior* does not actually deal with the text itself in terms of form criticism, literary criticism, or traditio-historical study, which are proper critical tools for investigation, but deals with later faith interpretations of the original text. What is of issue in the *sensus plenior* is the apparent failure to distinguish between the intended *content* of the text and the divine *purpose* of the text.[3] There are critical tools for the former, but not for the latter, which is what the *sensus plenior* is about.

The third proposed solution, that of Christocentrism, has been the most popular and the most perduring. Christocentrism, or as G. Ernest Wright prefers to call it, "Christomonism," "sharply restricts revelation to Jesus Christ, so that whatever is said about God is either confined to, or secondary to, what is said about Christ."[4] The limitations

of such a position become obvious when seen from the
perspective of the entire Bible.

In the first place, Christocentrism tends to be anti-Trinitarian by subordinating or minimizing the revelational activity of the Father and the Holy Spirit. The perspective of
the Old Testament points out very clearly the revelational
activity of God and his Spirit in the Creation, Exodus, and
other saving acts of history.

One significant source of this anti-Trinitarian Christocentrism has been our Christian pietistic heritage exempli-
fied in devotional hymns. Some of these hymns tended to
ascribe to Christ everything meaningful that one would
affirm about God, often blurring the distinction of function,
e.g., creation ascribed to Jesus in the hymn "O King of
Might and Splendor." [5] Likewise, the Divine Praises manifest a heavy Christocentrism that borders on the anti-Trinitarian. For example, there are two praises for God the
Father, five for Jesus, four for Mary, and one each for the
Holy Spirit, St. Joseph, and the combination of angels and
saints. This emphasis on Jesus and Mary tends to obscure
the role of the Father and the Spirit in the plan of salvation.

Secondly, Christocentrism tends to telescope history and
minimize the theological value of historical development
that is very much a part of the Old Testament. By attempting to see everything in the Old Testament as somehow
pointing to Jesus, we deprive the various events of the independent theological significance they had for their contemporaries, as well as the theological significance they
might have for us today.

A third difficulty with the Christocentric approach has
been its initial apologetic intent, which has led to the abuse

of "proof-texting." The early Christian community had experienced the unique event of Jesus and looked to the Old Testament as its chief resource for understanding the experience. Matthew saw Jesus as the new Moses and as the fulfillment of Old Testament prophecies. We see particularly in the early chapters of his Gospel the repeated formula, "All this took place to fulfill what was spoken by the prophet." A classic example of this apologetic statement is found in the account of the flight into Egypt culminating with the phrase in 2:15b, "This was to fulfill what the Lord had spoken by the prophet, 'Out of Egypt I have called my son.'" The prophet in question is Hosea, who, in his use of the phrase "out of Egypt I have called my son," in 11:1, referred to Israel's Exodus experience and not to Jesus' return to Palestine.

What can we conclude from this Christocentric approach that understands the Old Testament as apologetic statement? First of all, we can admit some legitimacy to this method in that any affirmation about the relationship between the Testaments is a faith judgment, and the boundaries of a faith judgment are set by the critical discipline of exegetical study. On the level of a faith affirmation a thing may be judged to be true if the parameters of analogy and imagery allow for it, i.e., if the conceptual framework for theological statement is linguistically acceptable. By contrast, on the level of critical exegesis, the limits of interpretation are clearly imposed on the text itself by means of more easily definable, objective criteria. Consequently, we could say of our illustration that when Matthew quoted the passage from Hosea, he was making a faith statement about Jesus and was not doing a critical exegesis of Hosea.

Secondly, we should allow the Old Testament to speak on its own terms to Christians, but not in terms defined by Christianity, so that the limits of Christocentrism can be recognized. One helpful way of allowing the Old Testament to speak for itself would be to respect what James Barr calls the "not yet." [6] That is to say, the Old Testament comes from the time when Jesus Christ had not yet come, and to expound it as if he had already come would be mistaken.

Finally, we come to the fourth of the proposed solutions, that of promise and fulfillment. The three positions described earlier—typology, *sensus plenior*, and Christocentrism—get at the problem of the relationship between the Testaments primarily through the notion of continuity, i.e., one works from the Old to the New Testament. On the other hand, the approach of promise-fulfillment can be considered from the viewpoints of both continuity and discontinuity. That is, continuity in the sense that the Old Testament contains the promise that is somehow fulfilled in the New, and discontinuity in the sense that the New Testament proposes an entirely new way of relating to God, namely, through the person Jesus. It is because of this dual approach of continuity and discontinuity that we have to properly understand what is meant by promise and fulfillment.

Promise is not prophecy, though prophecy may be promise. By emphasizing promise rather than prophecy in the promise-fulfillment dialectic, we are underscoring the wider historical conspectus of the former as well as its broader connection with fulfillment.

Walther Zimmerli understands promise in the Old Testament as a pledge, e.g., of land and posterity as promised to

Abraham in Genesis 12:1–3. The vitality of the promise-pledge comes in the fullness of blessing *(berakah)* which looks beyond the immediate and direct fulfillment of a given promise. Thus, blessing is seen as continuing fulfillment of the pledge-promise. Perhaps Zimmerli's idea is best expressed in his statement,

Every Old Testament event receives increasingly the character of a fulfillment which in turn presses the question of deeper fulfillment. All Old Testament history, insofar as it is history guided and given by Yahweh's word, received the character of fulfillment; but in the fulfillment it receives a new character as promise.[7]

What we have here is a statement that every fulfillment, in turn, becomes a promise awaiting further fulfillment. This idea of Zimmerli's has the twofold advantage of allowing for the constant expansion of the fulfillment idea, i.e., not limiting it to a specific promise at a specific time; and of understanding the necessary tension between promise and fulfillment in the context of *Heilsgeschichte*. It is in the understanding of this tension that options within the *Heilsgeschichte* become possible.

Claus Westermann speaks of a "*way* of promise through the Old Testament," by which he means a sketch of history which reaches from the deliverance from Egypt, Israel's historical beginning as God's people, to the apocalyptic of the late Israelite period. This history is not unilinear in that there is only one promise, but, as Westermann points out, there are several forms of the promise. From this, Westermann concludes that, "the final fulfillment of the promises of the Old Testament in the coming and the work of Christ can only be understood as a fulfillment of the *history* of the promises." [8] So, according to Westermann, it is only through an understanding of the total history of the promises that we can begin to grasp what fulfillment in the New Testament is all about.

In light of the above, what can we say about fulfillment? To begin with, we can say what it is not. It is not a matter of the New superseding the Old Testament, thereby rendering it meaningless. Neither is it an abstraction of uni-linear dimensions whereby the historical context is overlooked. Fulfillment can be several things. Some scholars speak of the biblical text as having a *Nachleben,* an afterlife, that forms part of its meaning.[9] That is, the biblical text during Israel's history was reinterpreted, e.g., the motif of marriage as model of relationship between Yahweh and Israel is seen in Hosea and in the Song of Songs. Two separate works were written at different times from different perspectives, yet they utilized the same theological reality.

Another way of employing the same notion of constant reinterpretation is to see developed understanding as an "interpretation continuum" in which an Old Testament text is understood differently according to context.[10] We acknowledge the importance of context concerning fulfillment when we see how, for example, Qumran and the New Testament understood the Old Testament. While both saw the Old Testament as having relevance, that the text had an ongoing life and meaning for the community, both saw the basis of fulfillment differently. For Qumran, fulfillment was in the future, i.e., in apocalyptic; and for the New Testament, fulfillment was in the past, i.e., in Jesus Christ.

There are at least two problems that surface in the whole

question of the promise-fulfillment schema, and both need serious investigation. They are the problem of the canon and the Jewish versus Christian understanding of the Old Testament. In the first place, if one posits a developing tradition and revelation in light of this broader understanding of fulfillment of promise, who then becomes its authoritative interpreter? A real investigation must be done into the meaning of the biblical community and its contemporary counterpart in order to properly understand the question of authority. The hierarchical model now in vogue obviously has severe limitations, and its assumption of a unilateral, definitive interpretation must be challenged in light of the biblical text itself.

Secondly, if we recognize that the Old Testament properly belongs to the Jews and only by historical and theological circumstance was appropriated by Christians, what then becomes of our assumption that Jesus fulfilled the Old Testament?[11] What justification do we have for terminating Old Testament traditions with the New Testament? Might not Jewish traditions help us to understand better what fulfillment of Old Testament promise is all about?[12]

As a suggestion for pushing forward critical reflection on fulfillment, I would like to pick up on Zimmerli's statement that "every Old Testament event receives increasingly the character of fulfillment which in turn presses the question of deeper fulfillment," and propose as a definition for fulfillment the following: "A contemporary faith judgment of the divine pledge interpreted in the light of a constant tradition." First, by *contemporary faith judgment* I mean a judgment that maintains the integrity of a theological assertion and comes under the rubric of what was earlier described as an interpretation continuum, which sees de-

velopment of meaning in the biblical text and postulates
that a fulfillment is neither static nor definitive. To be contemporary means to be flexible. To be flexible means to
take into account the social realities of the world around
us as part of the tradition. Flexibility in understanding fulfillment of promise was allowed by the early Church, e.g.,
Jude 14–15 quotes Enoch 1:9, and Jas. 4:5 and Eph. 5:14
quote unknown sources as authority. If we belong to the
same biblical community, why can't similar flexibility be
allowed us today? Ultimately, the contemporary judgment
is made by an individual within the context of a believing
and worshiping community, as was the case in the New
Testament where the Old Testament was not a problem for
the Apostles, but Jesus was, viz., how to understand him?

By *divine pledge* I mean the divine assurance of God's
promises in the context of the entire biblical history understood in the categories that are proper to that history.
By *in light of a constant tradition* is meant a tradition that
has very real ties with the Bible, and receives its truth from
it. The constancy of the tradition allows for both a radical
openness to the future and a flexibility of interpretation
such as we see in the New Testament.

In sum, one can understand fulfillment of promise as a
radical openness to the future which allows for several possibilities of interpretation, but is guided by a faith judgment that is consonant with the biblical traditions. Hence,
the need for critical exegesis as well as for flexibility. Thus
the success of understanding "fulfillment of promise" as a
theological category will depend on the degree of interaction between the subjectivity of a contemporary faith judgment and the objectivity of a constant tradition.

I have attempted to note that the question of Jesus and

the Old Testament is really a question of the relationship between the Testaments. It has been my contention that of the attempts to understand this relationship the most popular, the christocentric, has proven as unsuccessful as typology and the *sensus plenior*. Admittedly there is no single definitive solution, although the one that points to a more fruitful investigation is the promise-fulfillment schema. The focus has been intentionally on fulfillment, because fulfillment rather than promise or prophecy is the foundation of hope. For in fulfillment there is the continuous evaluation of the divine activity in history, which brings the assurance that God will keep his pledge of blessing to mankind as long as there is a personal response to the challenge of promise. In effect what I have been doing is making a plea for bringing the Old Testament out of its obscurity in the Christian experience. As Roland Murphy emphasized in his 1970 Bellarmine lecture:

The Church needs the Old Testament especially as a norm against which it is to measure itself. In this respect the writings of the New Testament, which are of course not to be neglected, often carry less impact. They deal with a relatively restricted period in the history of the Church, whereas the whole history of Israel is surveyed in the Old Testament. The point here is not that the theocracy of some particular Old Testament pattern is of special value, and so, a model. Rather the spiritual history of Israel, its fidelity and infidelity, the struggle of the people of God, the sense of election for service, those and other elements that are important for the life of the Church can come through more clearly and with greater effect by the use of the Old Testament rather than the New Testament.[13]

NOTES

[1] See his essay, "Typological Interpretation of the Old Testament," in Claus Westermann, ed., *Essays on Old Testament Hermeneutics* (Richmond: John Knox Press, 1963), pp. 17–39. (See also W. Eichrodt's essay, "Is Typological Exegesis an Appropriate Method?" in the same volume.)

[2] P. Benoit, J. Coppens, and R. Brown have been the strongest supporters of the *sensus plenior* in recent years. See R. Brown, "The *sensus plenior* in the Last Ten Years," *Catholic Biblical Quarterly* 25 (1963), pp. 262–285; "The Problems of the '*Sensus Plenior*'," *Ephemerides Theologiae Lovanienses* 43 (1967), pp. 460–469; "Hermeneutics," *Jerome Biblical Commentary*, vol. II, J. Fitzmyer and R. Murphy, eds., (Englewood Cliffs: Prentice-Hall, 1968), pp. 615–619. See an opposing view by Bruce Vawter, "The Fuller Sense: Some Considerations," *Catholic Biblical Quarterly* 26 (1964), pp. 85–96.

[3] There does not seem to be strong support for a *sensus* plenior outside of some Catholic circles.

[4] G. Ernest Wright, *The Old Testament and Theology* (New York: Harper & Row, 1969), p. 19. Wright makes a strong case for taking the Trinity seriously by taking the Old Testament seriously in theological study. With him I would understand Christocentrism not as every form of Christocentric piety and theology, but only as the severe narrowing of religious concern.

[5] *Maryknoll Missal* (New York: P. J. Kenedy and Sons, 1966), p. 608. Other examples abound.

[6] James Barr, *Old and New in Interpretation* (New York: Harper & Row, 1966), p. 152. Barr prefers the idea of "not yet" to that of "looks forward to" in the basic relationship between the Old Testament and the New Testament, since predetermination of divine intent can't be proved.

[7] "Promise and Fulfillment," in Westermann, *op. cit.*, p. 112.

[8] "The Way of the Promise through the Old Testament," in B. W. Anderson, ed., *The Old Testament and Christian Faith* (New York: Herder and Herder, 1969), p. 222. This volume contains excellent articles on the theological aspects of the problem between the Testaments, centering around Bultmann's crucial essay, which makes one of the strongest cases for discontinuity between the Testaments.

[9] Norbert Lohfink illustrates this well when he speaks of a "historical" and a "Christian" interpretation of the Old Testament. See his article, "Die historische und die chrislische Auslegung des Alten Testamentes," *Bibelauslegung im Wandel* (Frankfurt: Josef Knecht, 1967), pp. 185–213.

[10] Roland Murphy speaks of this "interpretation continuum." See his "Christian Understanding of the Old Testament," *Theology Digest* 18 (1970), pp. 321–332.

[11] James Barr has done a very sympathetic study of the problem in his "Le Judaïsme postbiblique et la théologie del'Ancien Testament," *Revue de Theologie et de Philosophie* Ser. 3, 18 (1968), pp. 209–217.

[12] See N. Lohfink, "Methodenprobleme zu eniem christlichen Traktat über die Juden," *Bibelauslegung im Wandel*, pp. 214–237.

[13] Murphy, *op. cit.*, p. 331.

Changing Concepts of God and Their Repercussions in Christology

BERNARD P. PRUSAK

In *Exodus* the Lord is described as "a God merciful and gracious, slow to anger, and abounding in steadfast love and faithfulness." [1] The Christian Scriptures speak of him as a kind God of love who sent his only son that we might live in a world of love, joy, and peace. [2] A problem arises when one tries to reconcile such language with the philosophical proclamation that God is "unchangeable" and "unaffected." Greek philosophers developed a notion of God which insisted upon his self-consistency: He never suffered passion or feeling. God was impassible (apathēs). His will was determined from within instead of being swayed from without. One might ask how such notions of God allow for his love to respond to our prayer. Qualities such as love and compassion hardly seem compatible with a self-sufficient infinite reality who possesses all he needs from all eternity and can never become, because he already is pure being. He cannot sympathize.

God is never called impassible in the Christian Scriptures. The term appears for the first time in the letters of Ignatius of Antioch. [3] After Justin Martyr the term becomes a standard part of Christian vocabulary. Robert M. Grant notes that the adoption of this attribute for God is paralleled by relatively few references to God's love in the subsequent writings of early Christians, especially in comparison with the Scriptures.[4]

Justin Martyr seems to have adopted his philosophical idea of God from Albinus of Smyrna, a Middle Platonist of the second century, whose world views and God concepts were an eclectic amalgam of Platonism and Aristotelianism. A brief review of the philosophical sources from which early Christianity drew its notion of God as impassible might clarify whether impassibility must be considered an essential and irrevocable attribute of the God of the Christians.

Plato accepted and distinguished between the two orders of Being and Becoming which Parmenides and Heraclitus had previously developed in isolation.[5] He identified the visible, tangible, material world perceived by the senses with the order of Becoming. In the *Republic* Plato explains that the visible world, subject to an endless procession of birth and decay in time and space, is but a shadow of a more substantial and unchanging reality called Being.[6] That is an immaterial order which is the realm of all intelligences and the rational part of human souls.

In the *Timaeus* the universe is described as a perfect sphere with the earth fixed in its center.[7] All the heavenly planets rotate about the earth at uniform speed in perfect circles. Such mathematically precise and unvarying circular motion is an activity of intelligent heavenly bodies which participate in the order of Being, and is therefore the visible, material embodiment of the unmoving perfection of a purely intelligible order, the realm of the Ideas. The most transcendent Idea, "the Good," is self-contained, pure being, approachable only through contemplation. It excludes all nonbeing, limitation, and the imperfection of becoming.[8] It seems to be in an order of its own, but is at the same time the universal source of all other being and intelligibility. Humans, who enjoy rationality, must expend the effort to overcome the passions that keep them tied to the bodily world of Becoming so that the rational and immortal part of their soul might by contemplation return to its native realm of Being.

Aristotle's world is much like Plato's.[9] His universe has an immobile earth surrounded by concentric, transparent spheres, which are like the layers of an onion. The innermost skin is the sphere of the moon. The possibility of change or incomplete motion (up and down, forward and back, right and left, generation and corruption) is limited to the space within that lunary sphere. Outside the sphere of the moon, the heavens are eternal and unalterable. The outermost layers of the onion-like universe are the spheres of the fixed stars which move in a perfect circle, the only complete or perfect motion. Beyond that is the realm of the Prime Mover who is absolutely unmoved: God.

In the *Metaphysics* Aristotle says that the First Mover causes change without itself being changed, without having any potentiality.[10] Aristotle's God is pure act (energeia), who causes the motion of the outermost sphere by final causality (by attracting, by drawing forth as the object of desire) and not by efficient causality (by pushing). The First Mover rules the world totally from the outside and really has no interaction with the world or humanity.

Aristotle maintains that it is wrong to think there can be a friendship towards such a God. In the *Magna Moralia* we read that God could not return our love and we could not in any case be said to love God.[11] A relationship of love with others outside himself is impossible for God since that would involve a becoming. "God cannot even have any object of thought outside himself, for that would mean that He had an end outside Himself. God, therefore, only knows himself." [12] He is an eternal act of self-consciousness which eternally thinks itself and nothing else.

Albinus combined Plato's universe with Aristotle's concept of a First God. God is the Unmoved Mover beyond the boundaries of the world who operates via final causality through the mediatorship of a World-Intellect.[13] The Platonic Ideas become eternal and changeless thoughts in the mind of God.[14] God is not a part of the world order but essentially different from it and the explanation for its existence. He is ineffable and can be grasped only by the intellect.[15]

Justin Martyr borrowed the Middle Platonic notion of divine transcendence as a means of rejecting the Stoic pantheism which threatened his Logos model for Jesus, his source of all wisdom and immortality.[16] The material nature of the Stoic God and his total immanence as world-reason (ὁ logos), the active *spirit* determining passive *matter*, posed a problem for Justin's identification of the *Logos* with Jesus Christ.[17] Rejecting the Stoics' pantheistic notion of Logos as the immanent divine consciousness or reason of a world constantly becoming and dissolving, Justin taught an incarnate Logos who always preserved his unity with a transcendent God the father by whom he was begotten for the purpose of creation and revelation.[18] Unfortunately, when Justin pragmatically used Middle Platonism's notion of a transcendent God to perfect his paradigm of Logos, he also introduced Aristotle's Unmoved Mover into Christianity.[19] (Actually, another apol-

ogist, Aristedes of Athens, preceded Justin in referring to
God as an Unmoved Mover.)[20]

In his commendable effort to oppose any identification
of a divine Logos with the world, Justin imported a notion
of God which originally allowed no relationship of love
between God and our world. Justin himself did not see any
incompatibility between a God of love and the Unmoved
Mover. He blended biblical images of God and philosophical concepts of God with an aplomb akin to that of the
Middle Platonists who blended Platonism and Aristotelianism.

Barnard believes that two conceptions of deity always
coexisted in Justin's mind since he could not articulate the
living and caring God of Christianity in intellectual terms.[21]
Alongside the biblical idea of God as a compassionate
Father who in Christ had drawn nearer to men and who
was concerned with the welfare of each soul,[22] Justin retained the Middle Platonist emphasis on God as the eternal
and unchangeable, impassible and transcendent Cause far
removed from the world and disconnected with it.[23] God
the Father remained on the other side of an impassable
chasm which allowed for no communication except through
the Logos. Those who became Christians (Christ-like)
would share God's very freedom from suffering and
death.[24]

While he termed God ineffable and nameless, Justin still
worshiped God as Father, prayed to him who sent salvation in Jesus, and admitted baptism in his name.[25] Justin
simply could not unite transcendence and immanence in
a system at once rational and biblical.[26] He and the other
apologists speak of a transcendent and immutable God

and at the same time of his relationship to the world which he created through his Word.[27]

Like Justin, Athenagoras also refers to "one God, un-created, eternal, invisible, impassible, incomprehensible, illimitable." [28] He too did not grasp the ambiguity which the negative Greek terminology concealed. Impassibility and immutability belong to the order of Being, which for the Middle Platonists could have nothing to do with the order of Becoming, our world. An impassible God of pure being is logically excluded and separated from the world of Becoming. Athenagoras' God is *apathēs*, totally unaffected by anything outside himself, and at the same time involved in our lives. According to Athenagoras God knows what we think and say so that if we live well here we are persuaded that we shall become impassible as he is:

We shall live another life, better than the present one, and heavenly, not earthly (since we shall abide near God, and with God, free from all change or suffering in the soul, not as flesh, even though we shall have flesh, but as heavenly spirit) . . .[29]

Athenagoras places little emphasis on God's love. God appears more as a judge.[30] Little is said of Jesus' human existence. The emphasis is on the Logos and his relationship to the Father.[31]

Irenaeus presupposes that it is impious to ascribe igno-rance and passion to the Father of all.[32] Furthermore, it necessarily follows that he who springs from the Father as Logos must be perfect and impassible.[33] At the same time, Irenaeus insists against the Docetists that Jesus truly suf-fered.[34] He fought and conquered. Through obedience he set free the weak and by destroying sin he brought salvation. Irenaeus rejects the gnostic position that it was impossible for the Savior to suffer since he was at once incomprehensible and invisible.[35] He also opposes Cerinthus, who held that the spiritual Christ departed from Jesus, who then suffered and rose again while Christ remained impassible because he was a spiritual being.[36]

Irenaeus maintains that God, the Father of all, is unproduced, unbegotten, incomprehensible, without figure or shape, never subject to passion (impassible), and never in error. He is unknowable except through the Son who came to declare him.[37] If the Gnostics had known the Scriptures they would have known that the Father of all is far removed from the emotions and passions that are common to men. "He is simple and uncompounded Being, without diversity of parts, altogether identical and self-consistent, since he is totally understanding, totally spirit, . . . totally hearing, seeing, and light, and the total source of all that is good." [38] Unmoved by anything, God freely fashioned Adam in the beginning not because he had need of man, but that he might have a being on whom he could bestow his benefits, which are salvation after sin, life, incorruption, and his own eternal glory.[39] Paradoxically, God is said not to need man but yet to want someone to love.

Irenaeus believes it is impossible to know God except by his love (for this it is which leads us to God by his Word).[40] Through his love and kindness God is knowable, not in his essence, which is beyond man, but as a creator who communicates with us.[41] God is good, merciful, and patient, saving those whom he ought to save. He is not unmercifully just because he is all goodness.[42] From reading such texts in Irenaeus it would seem that God's transcendent separation from the world and his unaffectability crumble before the power of his personal love for man.

Clement of Alexandria follows an already established tradition when he insists that God is impassible, free of anger, destitute of desire.[43] However, Clement also extended impassibility to the humanity of Jesus: "The image of God is the divine and royal Word, the impassible man."[44] According to Clement it would be ludicrous to suppose that the Savior's body demanded such essentials as food during his stay. Jesus didn't eat because his body needed food; it was sustained by a holy energy. Jesus ate food lest those around him fall into docetic notions about the reality of his bodily appearance.[45] "He was entirely impassible (apathēs), inaccessible to any movement of feeling—either pleasure or pain."[46] The followers of Jesus become impassible like their teacher:

. . . the apostles, having most gnostically mastered, through the Lord's teaching, anger, and fear, and lust, were not liable even to such of the movements of feeling as seem good, courage, zeal, joy, desire, through a steady condition of mind, not changing a whit; but ever continuing unvarying in a state of training after the resurrection of the Lord.[47]

Yet there are indications that Jesus' impassibility is not to be interpreted as if he were unaffected by other human beings. According to Clement, Jesus' impassibility guarantees his undivided care for us:

Nor does he ever abandon care for men, by being drawn aside from pleasure, who, having assumed flesh, which by nature is susceptible of suffering, trained it to the condition of impassibility.[48]

We are to believe in him who is God and man, who suffered and is worshiped as the living God.[49] Having admitted a God who cares and a Jesus who suffers, Clement's
stress on impassibility reveals some tensions.

Clement's emphasis on Jesus' unaffectability does not
simply reflect the stoic ideal of ethical apathy since it appears as an overflow of divine transcendence onto humanity. According to Clement, the impassible God cannot
be said to have emotions such as our joy or even our pity
for one who suffers undeservedly.[50] He rejoices without suffering change. God is totally distinct from us, having no
natural relation to us in his essence.[51] Both the Father and
Jesus are distinguished from us by the very uniqueness
of their impassibility.

At the same time Clement will simply presuppose that
God's mercy is rich to us who are the work of his will.[52] The
very fact that God cares for us, when by nature he is estranged from us, is the greatest proof of the goodness of
God. God's love and the suffering of his Son, Jesus, as an
expression of that love, really shatter philosophical transcendence. This is evidenced by a remarkable passage in
which Clement speaks of God becoming feminine through
his sympathy with us:

God is love and because of his love he pursued us. In his ineffable essence he is Father; in his compassion for us he became
mother. The Father by loving became feminine, and the great
proof of this is the Son whom he begot of himself and the love
that was the fruit brought forth by his love.

For this he came down. For this he clothed himself with
human nature. For this he voluntarily endured the sufferings
of man, that by bringing himself to the measure of our weakness he might raise us to the measure of his power. Just before

being offered up and giving himself as a ransom, he left us a new testament: I give you my love. . . . For each of us he gave his life, which was worth all there is, and he requires that we do the same for one another. . . . "Any one who hates his brother is a murderer." (1 John 3:15) . . . He has not God's compassion. He has no hope of better things. He is sterile and barren. He is not a branch of the everliving supercelestial vine.[53]

In Clement we have a very strange transcendence in comparison with that of the Greek philosophers; it admits of compassion and love which are expressed by assuming the possibility of suffering. The Son of God who supposedly never experienced real hunger suffered death out of his love for us.[54] The Son, who is the timeless and unoriginated First Principle, the beginning of existences, who without beginning was impassible, from whom we are to learn the remoter Cause, the Father, out of exceeding love for humanity took on human flesh, despising not its susceptibility to suffering.[55]

In his treatment of divine love Clement is really grappling with a new and totally different notion of transcendence, one which involves a different concept of becoming: "Through love, the future is already present for a Christian. . . . By love the Christian goes to meet the future." [56] The "being affected" which the relationship of love indicates need not be an imperfection but, at least in God, a perfection. However, Clement could not simply push aside the other notion of transcendence in which God was *essentially* estranged in his perfection as pure being. His God was at the same time loving and *essentially* unaffected.

In his Alexandrian period, Origen speaks of a transcendent God who is pure being and therefore completely

impassible, lacking all emotions.[57] Any biblical passages
which speak of God's joy or grief are to be considered
allegorical since he remains completely impassible.[58] However, Origen adds a new dimension to our discussion of
God's impassibility when he insists that one cannot think
of God without thinking of a "world" in which God's creative goodness is manifested and communicated.[59] There
never was a time when a world did not exist since God's
goodness always tends toward self-communication in an
infinite series of worlds.[60] God's immutability and the
eternal nature of his will also require an eternal creation.[61]

Origen did not stop with his realization that love requires that there be something loved. During his later
Caesarean period, which was more biblical in its emphasis,
Origen will remarkably admit that the Father and Savior
suffer the passion of love:

When I speak to a man and beg him to have pity on me in some
matter, if he is without compassion what I say to him causes
him no suffering; but if his feelings are tender and his heart is
not hard and callous, then he listens and has pity on me, and
his feelings are softened in response to my prayer. Something
of this sort I would have you suppose concerning the Saviour.
He came down to earth in pity for human kind, he endured our
passions and sufferings before he suffered the cross, and he
deigned to assume our flesh. For if he had not suffered he
would not have entered into full participation in human life.
He first suffered, then he came down and was manifested.
What is that passion which he suffered for us? It is the passion
of love. The Father himself and the God of the whole universe
is "longsuffering, full of mercy and pity" (Ps. 86:15). Must he
not then, in some sense, be exposed to suffering? So you must
realize that in his dealing with men he suffers human passions.

"For the Lord thy God bare thy ways, even as man bears his own son." Thus God bears our ways, just as the son of God bears our 'passions.' The Father himself is not impassible. If he is besought he shows pity and compassion; he feels, in some sort, the passion of love, and is exposed to what he cannot be exposed to in respect of his greatness, and for us men he endures the passions of mankind.[62]

Later theologians continued to grapple with the tension between philosophical impassibility and the revelation of God's love. Anselm, who is the gateway from the patristic era into the age of scholasticism, addresses himself to God about the problem in the *Proslogion:*

But how are You at once both merciful and impassible? For if You are impassible You do not have any compassion; and if You have no compassion Your heart is not sorrowful from compassion with the sorrowful, which is what being merciful is. But if you are not merciful whence comes so much consolation for the sorrowful?

How, then, are You merciful and not merciful, O Lord, unless it be that You are merciful in relation to us and not in relation to Yourself? In fact, You are (merciful) according to our way of looking at things and not according to Your way. For when You look upon us in our misery it is we who feel the effect of Your mercy, but You do not experience the feeling. Therefore You are both merciful because You save the sorrowful and pardon sinners against You; and You are not merciful because You do not experience any feeling of compassion for misery.[63]

Anselm does not go as far as the mellowed Origen. Since this study is not intended to be a survey we will not consider the later scholastics beyond noting that Aquinas tried

to interpret Aristotle in a manner which would not exclude
God's knowledge of the world and his providence. Following Augustine, Thomas says that God does not know the
world because he made it; rather, he first knew everything
in himself, as possible reflections of himself, which he then
created.[64] Yet, in taking the position that God became incarnate because man had sinned, Thomas seems to say that
what happens in the world does concern God.[65]

Scotus likewise deserves mention because, as we shall see
below, modern theology is indebted partly to him for its
insight that the Incarnation is the apex of creation and not
merely an act of restoration. However, contemporary
theologians do not simply accept Scotus' reasons for insisting that incarnation was always part of God's plan and
not merely occasioned by humanity's sin. For Scotus, God
could not be necessitated in his willing; only the *passible*
nature of Christ's coming might be due to the need for
redemption from sin.[66]

It is time to look at the question in a modern context. To
share the struggle of those previous to us is to make the
history of their problems part of our own personal history.
We sympathize with their creative realizations so that we
may grow beyond their solutions to new horizons. For that
reason we have tried to experience the dilemma of the
Fathers regarding a God who was utterly transcendent, impassible, and, at the same time, loving. If we have come
to understand the problem, the value of some contemporary responses should be more easily appreciated.

We have gradually set aside the Greek philosophers'

notions of the universe. Copernicus and Galileo removed the earth from the center. Kepler discovered that the motion of the celestial bodies is elliptical and not perfectly circular. Newton's insights regarding gravity and the tendency of bodies in motion to stay in motion eliminated the need for Aristotle's First Mover who, as a Final Cause, effected the circular motion of the intelligent outermost sphere. Darwin's theory of evolution established the idea that the world is not static but enjoys a process of growth into greater perfection. After Einstein the ultimate foundation of physical reality is seen to involve relationships. Because the very worldviews which originally excluded any possible relationship with God have all but disappeared, some new options are possible in talking about God. To speak of him as love is to define him by his personal relationships. He transcends in his relationships and not by any absolute exclusion of them.

When Karl Rahner asks what is the meaning of the assertion, "the Word of God has *become* man," he encounters the very problem which puzzled the ancients. "The acknowledgement of the unchanging and unchangeable God in his eternally perfect fullness is not merely a postulate of philosophy, it is also a dogma of faith. Nonetheless, it remains true the Word *became* flesh." [67]

Faced with the fact of the Incarnation, which he recognizes as the fundamental dogma of Christianity, Rahner finds that he must say: "God can become something, he who is unchangeable in himself can *himself* become subject to change in something else." [68] Revelation brings us to an ontological ultimate which a purely rational ontology might not even suspect or find it difficult to accept. For Rahner, God's transcendence as Creator is a derivative possibility ultimately based on the primal possibility of God's love.[69] He is love, which wills to fill the void and so creates the other. God is most essentially a fullness which gives itself away, and becomes in the other, without having to change in its own proper reality, which is the unoriginated origin. God is most essentially a fullness which gives itself away, empties itself, but always has just as much to give.

Rahner accepts Scotus' position that the event of Jesus would have taken place in creation even without sin, but for his own reasons: "The historical person whom we call Saviour is that subjectivity in whom this process of God's absolute self-communication to the spiritual world is *irrevocably* present as a whole." [70] Jesus, who is the Logos become material, is the self-communication of God, whose relationship with history introduces the possibility of conscious and free self-transcendence into the process of the world becoming.[71] As Metz would say, Jesus is God's acceptance of the world as "other" in a relationship of love which frees the "other" to realize its potentialities.[72] Although Rahner's philosophical presuppositions are different than those of process thinkers his ideas on "God becoming" in the Incarnation seem to move him into a position compatible with certain ideas of Whitehead and Hartshorne.

The tender elements in the world which slowly and in quietness operate by love attracted the attention of Alfred North Whitehead.[73] Love, which neither rules nor is unmoved, became the starting point for his theistic philosophy: It is precisely love which must be perfect in God. Somewhat like Origen, whose notion of God's goodness presupposed an eternal creation, Whitehead could not think of God without relating him to a world in which his created goodness is concretized. His God is dipolar, having a primordial and a consequent nature.[74] "Viewed as primordial, he is the unlimited conceptual realization of the absolute wealth of potentiality." [75] "His unity of conceptual operations is a free creative act, untrammelled by reference to any particular course of things." [76] The particularities of the actual world presuppose the primordial nature of God, which nature of God merely presupposes the *general* metaphysical character of creative advance, of which it is the primordial exemplification.

The primordial side of God's nature is free, complete, and eternal but *actually* deficient and unconscious. The consequent nature of God is determined, incomplete, consequent, "everlasting," fully actual, and conscious.[77] It originates with physical experience derived from the temporal world, and then acquires integration with the primordial side. God becomes actualized with the concrescence of the world becoming.

For Whitehead, God is the infinite ground of all mentality, the unity of vision seeking physical multiplicity. The world is the multiplicity of finites, actualities seeking a perfected unity.[78] "God and the World are the contrasted opposites in terms of which Creativity achieves its supreme task of transforming disjoined multiplicity, with its diversities in opposition, into concrescent unity, with its diversities in contrast." [79]

Whitehead sees the universe as pluralist; its elements are not independent but related. It consists of an infinite and related number of occasions for becoming, each of which draws on being in a process which is the endless realization of potentialities.[80] Every individual reality is a potentiality for *being* an element in a new synthesis of endless *becoming*. The already actual can always become new when it moves toward a goal. However, one must be careful not to simply identify the world with becoming and flux, and God with being and permanence.[81] The world might protect its being, the present status quo, unless it were lured toward concretizing a new subject and ideal by an underlying energy of realization which is creativity. As the "lure for feeling, the eternal urge of desire," God is the source of becoming who overcomes the world's compulsion with the static present by the persuasive lure of what might be.[82] God creates the world in a persuasive manner offering to each occasion its possibilities of value. "The consequent nature of God is the fluent world become everlasting by its objective immortality in God." [83] God offers the world permanence in the primordial unity of his vision and derives his flux from the world. According to Whitehead, neither God nor the world reaches static completion. He presupposes that both are in the grip of the ultimate metaphysical ground, the creative advance into novelty. God and the world are the instruments of novelty for one another.[84]

In his reflections on Whitehead's dipolar notion of God, Charles Hartshorne has pointed out that God's perfection must be defined in a way that includes supreme sensitivity, sympathetic dependence, and the possibility of his self-surpassing experience of new value. He must enjoy our joy and grieve with our sorrows.[85] God's abstract, absolute side is balanced by a concrete, relative side. Both of these are aspects of a concrete and dynamic reality who is related to the world by his love and compassion.[86]

Both Whitehead and Hartshorne have shifted the philosophical consideration of God away from the notions of his omnipotence as a creator who has control *over* a world which he necessarily transcends, to his ongoing creative relationship of love *with* a world in process. Rather than exclude God from the world they include the world in their notion of God.[87] The panentheism which Hartshorne proposes includes the world in a God who is more than world, and in that sense transcendent.[88] God is distinguished from the world but at the same time is interiorly modified and manifests himself in relation with the world. As Rahner and Vorgrimler say, God and the world are the reciprocal conditioning of unity and difference growing in the same proportion. "This doctrine of the 'immanence' of the world in God is false and heretical only if it denies creation and the distinction of the world from God (and not only of God from the World)." [89] What happens in the world affects God who in turn affects the world. God's love passes into the world. The love in the world passes into God and floods back again into the world. "In this sense, God is the great companion—the fellow-sufferer who understands." [90]

In another place we have previously considered the entire event of Jesus' life and death as the concrete and saving revelation that it is safe to love, to be affected by others' needs, to be vulnerable to becoming something new in one's relationships even at the greatest risk.[91] Jesus is the decisive example of what God is always about: love which gives itself to the other that he or she may find worth as an individual and pass on the love. As the divine way of being man, Jesus leads us to the realization that God is love, the epitome of concern and sensitivity who empathizes with the others to whom he is open and with whom it is part of his very nature to be involved. Because God cares, he suffers and shares our struggle when we fear to take the

risk of living freely and of becoming ever new in our relationships with one another. If anything is immutable in
God it is the completeness of his love for us, which must
include responses to our everchanging needs.

NOTES

[1] 34:6 (Revised Standard Version).

[2] See *Lk.* 6:35; *John* 3:16; 1 *John* 4:8–11; 2 *Cor.* 13:13; *Gal.* 2:20 and
5:22.

[3] *Epistle to Polycarp* 3:2 and *Ephesians* 7:2. Both passages refer to the
divinity of Christ. Immutability is attributed to God in *Malachi* 3:6 and
James 1:17.

[4] *The Early Christian Doctrine of God* (Charlottesville, Va.: University
of Virginia Press, 1966), pp. 4–5.

[5] See *Sophist* 249d, 3–4.

[6] Book 9, 585c–d; *Laws* Bk.10, 893–894.

[7] See 30–52.

[8] See *Republic,* 507b–509b.

[9] See *De Caelo,* Bk. 2, 3–14: 286a–98a 20; Bk. 1, 2 & 3: 268b 11–270b
30; Bk. 3, 1: 298a 24–298b 33. *De Generatione et Corruptione,* Bk. 2, 9:
335a 24–25. *Physics,* Bk. 4, 14: 223a 29– 224a 2.

[10] Book Lambda, chapters 6–9: 1071b– 1075a. (Chapter 8, which refers
to 55 or 47 movers seems a later insertion. Even then Aristotle admits that
a multiplicity of movers raises a problem to which he offers no solution:
1074a 35–36.) See also *Physics,* Bk. 8, 1–10: 250b 10– 267b 25.

[11] 1208b 26–32.

[12] Frederick Copleston, *A History of Philosophy,* vol. 1, *Greece and
Rome* (Westminster, Md.: Newman Press, 1950), pp. 316–317. See also
Aristotle, *Metaphysics,* Book ʌ, 9: 1074b 33–35.

[13] *Didaskalikos* 10, 2. Our references are to the edition of the *Épitomé,*
ed. Pierre Louis (Paris: Société d'Édition "Les Belles Lettres," 1945).

[14] *Didaskalikos* 9, 1; 9, 3; and 10, 3.

[15] *Didaskalikos* 10, 4.

[16] 2 *Apology* 7.

[17] "Like Heraclitus the Stoics make fire to be the stuff of all things.
God is the active fire (*material but of a finer stuff*) which is immanent in
the universe, but He is at the same time the primal Source from which

the crasser elements, that make the corporeal world, come forth." Copleston, *op. cit.*, p. 388. God is the soul and consciousness, the moving and forming principle of the coarser corporeal stuff of which the world is formed. He forms the world in which he is immanent as reason and then takes it back into himself through a universal conflagration. There are an unending series of world-constructions and world-destructions.

[18] 1 *Apol.* 64; 2 *Apol.* 6; *Dialogue* 84.

[19] *Dialogue* 127.

[20] *Apology* 1.

[21] L. W. Barnard, *Justin Martyr: His Life and Thought* (Cambridge: Cambridge University Press, 1967), pp. 79 and 83.

[22] Cf. in order: *Dialogue* 108; 1 *Apol.* 28 and 37; 1 *Apol.* 10; 2 *Apol.* 4 & 6; and *Dialogue* 1.

[23] Cf. 1 *Apol.* 13, 4 and *Dialogue* 3; 5; and 127; 1 *Apol.* 25, 2; 2 *Apol.* 7.

[24] *Dialogue* 124, 4 and 2 *Apol.* 1, 2.

[25] See 1 *Apol.* 9, 3; 10, 1; 61; 2 *Apol.* 12; 13; *Dialogue* 127; 1 *Apol.* 22; 2 *Apol.* 13 and 1 *Apol.* 6; 13; 61.

[26] Barnard, *op. cit.*, p. 84.

[27] Justin: 1 *Apol.* 10, 2; 13, 1; *Dialogue* 56, 1; 3, 5; 4, 1; 59; 61; and 2 *Apol.* 6 (It is not clear whether Justin held a creation out of nothing or out of a formless matter.); Aristides: *Apology* 15, 3; Athenagoras: *Supplicatio* 4 and 6; Tatian: *Oratio* 5, 1–3; Theophilus of Antioch: *Ad Autolycum* 1, 5.

[28] *Supplicatio* 10, 1; see also 8, 2.

[29] *Ibid.*, 31, 3. Unless otherwise noted, translations are from *The Ante-Nicene Fathers*, eds. A. Roberts and J. Donaldson, revised by A. Cleveland Coxe (New York: Scribner's, 1899).

[30] *Ibid.*, 31 and 36.

[31] *Ibid.*, 10.

[32] *Adversus Haereses* 2, 17, 6.

[33] *Ibid.*, 2, 17, 7.

[34] *Ibid.*, 3, 18, 6.

[35] *Ibid.*, 1, 7, 2. According to Irenaeus, Jesus who suffered for us was the Word made man, "the invisible becoming visible, the incomprehensible being made comprehensible, the impassible becoming capable of suffering. . . ." *Ibid.*, 3, 16, 6.

[36] *Ibid.*, 1, 26, 1.

[37] *Ibid.*, 4, 6, 3.

[38] *Ibid.*, 2, 13, 3. (Rendering is mine.)

[39] *Ibid.*, 4, 14, 1.

[40] *Ibid.*, 4, 20, 1.

[41] *Ibid.*, 3, 24, 2.

[42] *Ibid.*, 3, 25, 3

[43] *Stromata* 4, 23.

[44] *Ibid.*, 5, 14.

[45] *Ibid.*, 6, 9.

[46] *Ibid.*

[47] *Ibid.*

[48] *Ibid.*, 7, 2.

[49] *Protrepticus* 10. Clement further adds that God in his love for man comes to his aid as a mother-bird flies to one of her young that has fallen out of its nest; "the mother flutters round, uttering cries of grief" (*Iliad* 2, 315).

[50] *Stromata* 2, 16.

[51] C. *Stromata* 7, 14: "For we do not say, as the Stoics do most impiously, that virtue in man and God is the same. Ought we not then to be perfect, as the Father wills? For it is utterly impossible for any one to become perfect as God is."

[52] *Ibid.*, 2, 16.

[53] *Quis Dives Salvetur?* 37. (Rendering is mine.)

[54] *Ibid.* and *Stromata* 6, 8.

[55] *Stromata* 7, 1 & 2.

[56] *Ibid.*, 6, 9.

[57] *De Principiis* 2, 4, 3 and 4 and 1, 1, 5–7; *Contra Celsum* 7, 38.

[58] *Homily on Numbers* 23, 2. (Regarding God's impassibility cf. *Homily on Numbers* 16, 3 which is an interpretation of *Numbers* 23, 19.)

[59] *De Principiis* 3, 5, 3; 2, 9, 6; and 4, 4, 8.

[60] *Ibid.* 3, 5, 3; 1, 4, 3. (See also 2, 1, 3 and 2, 3, 4–5.) In *De Principiis*, preface, 7, Origen concedes the Church's teaching that our present world was created and began to exist at a definite time. However, in his opinion, that does not exclude other worlds before and after ours.

[61] See *De Prin.* 1, 2, 10.

[62] *Hom. in Ezechielem* 6, 6. Trans. Henry Bettenson, *The Early Christian Fathers* (New York: Oxord University Press, 1969), pp. 186–187. Origen had already written that the impassible Son suffered by being compassionate (*Matt. comm.* 10, 23).

[63] Chapter 8. Text from the edition by M. J. Charlesworth (Oxford: Clarendon Press, 1965), pp. 124–125.

[64] For Augustine see *De Genesi ad Litteram* 5, 15, 33; *Ad Orosium* 8, 9; *De Trinitate* 15, 7, 13. For Thomas see *In XII Libros Metaphysicorum* 12, lect. 11.

[65] *Summa Theologiae* III 1, art. 3.

[66] *Opus Oxoniensis, On the Sentences* 3, dist. 7, q. 3, nn. 3–5; dist. 19, quaestio unica, scholium n. 6; and dist. 20, quaestio unica, scholium nn. 8–10.

[67] "On the Theology of the Incarnation," in *Theological Investigations,* vol. IV: *More Recent Writings* (Baltimore: Helicon Press, 1966), p. 112.

[68] *Ibid.,* p. 113.

[69] *Ibid.,* p. 115. On page 114 Rahner maintains that the basic element of God, according to our faith, is the *self-emptying,* the coming to be.

[70] Karl Rahner, "Christology within an Evolutionary View of the World," in *Theological Investigations,* vol. V: *Later Writings* (Baltimore: Helicon Press, 1966), pp. 175 and 184–185.

[71] *Ibid.,* pp. 173–192.

[72] Johannes B. Metz, *Theology of the World* (New York: Herder and Herder, 1969), pp. 25–32. See also Daniel Day Williams, *The Spirit and the Forms of Love* (New York: Harper and Row, 1968), chapter 6.

[73] Alfred North Whitehead, *Process and Reality: An Essay in Cosmology* (New York: Macmillan, 1929, sixth reprint 1967), p. 520.

[74] *Ibid.,* p. 524.

[75] *Ibid.,* p. 521.

[76] *Ibid.,* p. 522.

[77] *Ibid.,* p. 524.

[78] *Ibid.,* p. 529.

[79] *Ibid.,* p. 528.

[80] *Ibid.,* pp. 27–28, 53, 101–104, 320–323, and 530.

[81] *Ibid.,* p. 528.

[82] *Ibid.,* pp. 522, 129–131, 46–48, 104, 248, 342–343.

[83] *Ibid.,* p. 527.

[84] *Ibid.,* p. 529.

[85] *Man's Vision of God and the Logic of Theism* (Hamden, Connecticut: Archon Books, 1964), pp. 22–24, 46–47. ". . . what one cannot do is to fail . . . to derive at least some value from the joys (of others) through the act of recognition itself, and precisely the most perfect mind would derive most from the satisfactions of others" (pp. 22–23). See also *The Divine Relativity: A Social Conception of God* (New Haven: Yale University Press, 1948 and 1964, reprinted 1967), pp. 20, 42–51, 54–56, 136, 141, and 148.

[86] *Man's Vision of God,* pp. 50–51 and 230–250: "The Divine Self-Creation"; *The Divine Relativity,* pp. 26, 30–32, 40, 52–53, 80–83, 86–88, 120–124, 142–146, 156–157.

[87] "The consequent nature of God is the fluent world become 'everlasting' by its objective immortality in God . . . God is completed by the

individual, fluent satisfactions of finite fact . . ." Whitehead, *Process and Reality*, p. 527.

[88] See *Man's Vision of God*, p. 348; *The Divine Relativity*, pp. 88–92; "Introduction: The Standpoint of Panentheism" and "The Logic of Panentheism" in *Philosophers Speak of God*, ed. Charles Hartshorne and William L. Reese (Chicago: University of Chicago Press, 1953), pp. 1–25 and 499–514.

[89] Karl Rahner and Herbert Vorgrimler, "Panentheism," in *Theological Dictionary* (New York: Herder & Herder, 1965), pp. 333–334. Cf. Denz. 1782.

[90] Whitehead, *Process and Reality*, p. 532.

[91] Bernard P. Prusak, "Toward a Theology of Vulnerability: The Liberating Embrace of the Human Condition," in *A World More Human, A Church More Christian*, ed. George Devine (Staten Island, N.Y.: Alba House, 1973), pp. 9–26.

PART II

THE DIFFERENCE JESUS MAKES

The Uniqueness of Jesus in Christian Tradition

Anyone teaching Christian theology to college students or
adults today is liable to be swept out of his professional
cool and into a vortex of uncharted chaos rather rapidly
with the question: What difference does Jesus make? After
the death and the subtle resuscitation of God, after secu-
larization and the renewed feasting of the surviving fools,
after linguistic analysis and the rebirth of myth and magic,
what are we to make of the questions: In what way is
Jesus unique? Could anyone have been the Christ or in
what sense is this predetermined? Why should it be impossible that another Christ arise? In what sense is Jesus
universal mediator? Do not Jews and others in fact move
towards the reign of the transcendent God without this
mediation?

These questions do not easily remain "theirs" but in-
eluctably become "ours." When I have addressed these
questions to my theological friends I have found that they
answered far more with their lives than they were able to
answer with their words. When I have turned with these
questions to the writings of Rahner and Ratzinger, Schil-
lebeeckx, Schoonenberg and Smulders, Pannenberg, Mey-
endorff, Bornkamm and others, I have found the answers

81

always somewhat short of the questions. This, of course, is not in itself a state of abnormality but it is very different from what we had been led to expect.

It is my thesis in this essay that we may have more resources for an ongoing creative Christology than we commonly acknowledge in theological discourse today. It has been pointed out by various authors[1] that along with the Christology elaborated out of the Chalcedonian definition (which has tended to be static and more and more remote from questions concerning the Christian way of life), we have a constantly developing redemption theology that has reflected the changing experience and understanding of the Christian community, and which functions in effect as an alternate approach to Christology.

It has also been pointed out[2] that the Chalcedonian formulation is not as dead or inflexible as it is frequently presented to be. Nor is it entirely irrelevant to the questions being asked today.

However, to explore only these two lines of development would be to ignore almost the whole body of tradition concerning the uniqueness of Jesus. That body of tradition consists not only of formal credal statements and their systematic expositions, but of legends and folktales, miracle and apparition stories, songs, prayers and iconography. Though certainly allowing for more ambiguity, the language of piety is a more fundamental level of the tradition than the language of a systematic theology, which is after all, based upon the former. When we look to our tradition for resources to tackle the contemporary christological questions, the iconography and devotional literature concerning the Sacred Heart, for example (whether or not we of today consider it to be in good taste) represents a most significant testimony concerning the uniqueness of Jesus as seen by Christians.[3]

Moreover, we cannot be content with verbal and graphic formulation, because we have at our disposal a yet more fundamental level of the tradition in the testimony of Christian lives and, of course, Christian deaths. We not only have the simple testimony that particular Christians lived thus and so in pursuit of their understanding of the promise and the vision held out by Jesus. We have further evidence in the tradition that the community of believers spontaneously singled out certain persons for admiration and imitation, apparently with intuitive recognition that the interpretation given in these lives as to why and how Jesus makes a difference, rang true.

Beyond such spontaneous recognition, we also have the testimony of the voice of authority speaking within the Church community, canonically sanctioning such admiration and imitation in specific instances and authorizing shrines, pilgrimages, devotional practices and festivals.[4] Characteristically, within the Catholic tradition, we have inserted the reflection on these lives and deaths within the Eucharistic celebration as part of the texts for meditation that should illuminate the meaning of Jesus' death for us in our times "until he comes."

We have, therefore, not only a more or less random sampling of expressions of what difference Jesus makes to certain persons, but we have a process within the community of believers of weighing and authenticating these expressions, which should most certainly be taken with the utmost seriousness in the contemporary task of building a viable and orthodox Christology. This paper offers some consideration of the way this level of testimony from the tradition might be used.

In order to project such a task, however, one is really required to ask oneself: How much do we expect of the past as past? Does Christian theology expect to find in the past already formulated answers to the questions of today? In order to make an authentic statement concerning the meaning of Jesus, must I show my statement to be explicit or at least implicit in the New Testament writings, or in the ancient creeds, or in the conciliar definitions of the great councils of antiquity, or at least in some magisterially sanctioned statement somewhere? Or must I be able to show that it follows as a logical necessity out of the prayer and practice of the Church in the past?

One might answer these questions various ways. In contemporary theology there seems often to be an unrestrained use of speculation based on attempts to analyze the human condition in general, but on the other hand very little tolerance for the creative imaginings of Christian piety expressed concretely in the community of Jesus' followers.[5] This creates several problems. The so-called "human condition in general" turns out to be an elitist, culturally biased, heavily class-conscious pattern of introspection that is no more universal than the professorial ranks of certain Western universities. Moreover, it is not evident that the analysis of the human condition in general —if such a project were really possible—could shed more light on the difference that Jesus makes than an analysis of the varied testimonies of those who have devoted their lives to the implications of what they perceived to be that difference.

Allowing for the necessary epistemological sophistication, and the necessary critical awareness of the nature of
our early sources, the proper answer to the questions enu-
merated above would seem to be in terms of the spirit in
the Church. There cannot be a line drawn across history
to mark the point at which the experience of the community has reached maturity and has been adequately
formulated, so that thereafter Christian theology takes its
point of departure from the formulation without need of
further consulting the faithful in matters of doctrine.[6] But
neither, as we decided in the heyday of gnosticism, can
there be a line drawn through the community of believers,
separating those who "know" and whose experience counts,
from those other ordinary people whose experience does
not count. The Christian, though not the humanitarian,
meaning of Jesus, very quickly falls apart without the doctrine of the spirit in the Church, that is without the assumption that the deeper meaning of Jesus as the Christ is
discovered by the community of his followers in their continuing effort through the ages to live out the implications
of the meaning that they already see.

A generation or so ago there was a great effort, led by
men such as Garrigou-Lagrange, to put the traditional
spiritual theology of Catholicism on a sound doctrinal basis.
It would seem that the time is more than ripe for a con-
certed effort to put the traditional doctrinal theology on its
sound spiritual basis. Moreover, to be sound, that basis
simply must be wider than the spiritual perception of university professors with their particular cultural and intellectual bias.[7] To achieve that width, in view of the com-
plexity and plurality of Christian experience after nineteen
centuries, not only a simple conversion of heart but a very

arduous conversion of mind seems to be required. Among other things, it suggests that the methodical process of theologizing must be far less after the model of philosophy and far more after the model of some of the newer human sciences in which the concern is not with statistics but with the discovery of coherent patterns or configurations of experience, behavior and meaning in the life of a person or community.[8]

If we search in this manner for an understanding of the uniqueness of Jesus and its formulation in Christian tradition, we are immediately confronted with the need for criteria in evaluating the testimonies. It is clear that such criteria cannot be derived from an appeal to "factual information" behind or prior to the subjective experience. By this time, the critical study of Scripture and the careful inquiry into Christian origins have made it quite clear that what we know of Jesus is the impact he has had on believers at various times, most of all in his own time. There is no appeal beyond the testimony of the impact he had, to further information ontological or psychological, concerning the inner reality of Jesus, by which the perceptions of believers might be judged or corrected. All doctrinal statements and all dogmatic formulations are the outcome of communal reflection on the various efforts to express the impact that Jesus has had on his followers—no more than that but certainly also no less, for a formulation based on such reflection is enormously important, the more so when it originally was, or subsequently became, a formulation universally accepted by the churches.

If we are serious in seeking an understanding of the uniqueness of Jesus in its formulation in Christian tradition, then the great credal statements of Nicea and Con-

stantinople, Ephesus and Chalcedon, are certainly not to
be dumped out with the trash. They have to be seen in
relation to the Christian spirituality which produced them.
It is not necessary or helpful to ignore the political in-
trigue, the unworthy motivations, the contentious factions
that played so great a role in the early councils, but it is
also ludicrous to focus on these as the basic formative influences, denying the role of spirit in the Church and yet
claiming to be doing Christian theology.

The criteria for evaluating the testimonies, therefore,
may arise out of doctrinal formulations, not however as
though these were prior to Christian experience and derived from an independent source, but because they are
already part of the ongoing flow of Christian experience
through the centuries—moments when the community of
believers has stopped, reflected on its experiences, and
wrestled with a mixture of fair motives and foul to come to
terms with the truth in the conflicting testimonies. This
process, which we can now study in retrospect, offers some
important insights into the possibilities of dealing with the
conflicting testimonies in Christian experience today. It
does not eliminate the necessity of our coping with today's
questions on the basis of today's Christian experience
evaluated by the cumulative reflection and wisdom of the
community's past experience.

The experience of the early councils tells us, for instance
in the formula of Chalcedon, that it may be necessary to
accommodate conflicting testimonies in a more or less paradoxical formulation, without resolving the difference between them because the spirituality and traditions out of
which they are offered both ring true.[9] The process by
which, in retrospect, these particular councils and not

others became the classic councils of antiquity tells us that whether we intend it or not, those formulations become central in the tradition which effectively acts as a rallying point for the Christian understanding of the meaning of Jesus—whether or not they are understood in the sense originally intended, or in the sense that scholarship surmises was originally intended.

The process leading up to the early councils also strongly suggests criteria for the evaluation of testimonies which do not depend on the verbal conformity of these testimonies to agreed dogmatic formulations. The words of martyrs for the faith are treasured above all in the practice of the early Church, and beyond this it would seem that a Christian has the right to be heard in the Church on two grounds—the familial piety with which he has treasured the testimony handed down from the Apostles, and the extent of his personal investment in the following of Jesus as measured by persecution and renunciation.[10] These two standards seem to be continued beyond the patristic era in the canonical recognition of doctors and saints, though the criteria for such recognition are less obvious when applied after the era of the great dogmatic formulations and after the era of persecution within an established Christendom. Nevertheless, such criteria are important to identify.

Confronted with many contemporary and historical testimonies of what Jesus means to various people, or what difference Jesus makes, one must indeed ask in each case how seriously the testimony is worth a hearing. The criteria will always in one way or another return to the two standards mentioned. The evaluation cannot rest simply on philosophical coherence, nor even on extensive scholarly analysis of the texts of Scripture. It must also take into account whether the testimony comes from one who has entered into the one organically unified event of Christian revelation by cherishing what was handed down from those who knew Jesus in the flesh—both what was handed down in the Scriptures and what has emerged from the developing life of the community through the ages.

Moreover, any evaluation of testimonies must take into account the extent to which the witness knows the scene as a participant, the experience from within, in terms of his personal investment in it. Through the centuries a pattern has emerged in the way in which the Catholic Church has canonized saints and in which all communions have identified their Christian heroes. The primacy and universality of charity have, of course, been the hallmark. But more specifically, the concern to identify with the oppressed, the poor, the disadvantaged, the forgotten, the condemned, the losers, the unimportant, and to extend to them the promises of the reign of God, is what in retrospect on a life-testimony we have always recognized as the watermark of the true witness. It is evidently from such sources that we may look for new insight in Christology today.

What, then, are the resources we have in the traditional formulations of the uniqueness of Jesus? From the beginning we have realized: in this man, uniquely, God speaks to us, speaks to us an inexhaustible utterance, an utterance that can be heard and reflected indefinitely without coming to the end of it. And, consciously playing on the many meanings of the term, we have identified Jesus as the Word of God, the Word that God utters from the beginning, the Word that expresses God himself, the Word that is intrinsically divine. It is a small step to say that the

Word that Jesus is essentially precedes his time in history, is uttered in the transcendent God, is uttered in eternity. It is another small step to say that the Word of God which we have heard concretely spoken in history in Jesus, which is that Word already uttered in eternity, is that communication of the ultimate, that design for the universe, for which men of other traditions are listening, conjecturing that it must be there.

From the beginning, our Christology suffered the temptation to depart for eternity and the absolute, and simply to abandon the historical and the human. We have had to take stock from time to time, and to recall the sweat and the blood and tears and the corpse, not simply for historical accuracy but to remember that we were speaking of the human—what has come about and must come about, not only on our behalf but within and among us. We had to remember not only that the Word of God of which we spoke was body, accessible to sight and touch, become concrete and experiential for us in history, but that the Word of God that was the divine utterance was human, uttered in the reflexive self-awareness that is the source of human freedom.

In the patristic era we hammered out this understanding into great dogmatic formulations. In the medieval era we came by it anew and painfully in the endless devotions dwelling on the various sufferings of Jesus in his passion as well as those surrounding his infancy and concerning Mary, his mother—a devotional history of which we are perhaps too quick to be ashamed and embarrassed today. In both cases, our consciousness has been that of difficult paradox in the convictions expressed, but this is because our experience of being human and our conception of God is such that we see the freedom that is God and the freedom that is man as necessarily oppositional.

Using the formulation of Jesus as the eternal Word of God who is, therefore, by nature both divine and human, we have been able to contain the paradox arising out of our immature human experience and immature concepts of God. We have acknowledged that immaturity precisely when we designated Jesus the Adam of the end-time, of the fulfillment of mankind's historical vocation. By this term we have acknowledged in effect that the conflict we experience does not belong in the relation between man and God, and that we see Jesus rather than ourselves as the norm of the truly human.[11]

We have not remained only with the image of the Word. Faced with the difficulty of imagining an utterance that is not subsequent to him who utters it, a word that is not other than the speaker but of the self-same reality, we have used other explosive images such as the shining of light, Light from Light.[12] These formulas and images can be and surely should be meditatively, imaginatively elaborated by Christian piety in all times including our own, rather than taken over as though they had scientific precision or clearly defined and static meaning. Yet, when all is said and done, this is the easy part of Christology. The difficult part comes when we try to establish the content of this word that has been uttered to us.

From the beginning, in answer to the question of what exactly is this difference that Jesus makes, Christians have said without hesitation that it is the difference between total despair and unquenchable hope. When asked how he makes this difference, they have answered with equal

alacrity that it is by his death, from which God has raised
him. In response to the question as to what then is the
meaning of his death, which may also be formulated simply
as the question concerning why he died, the answers are
no longer as terse or univocal. It is around this question
that we have built another whole approach to Christology
that has been by no means static or uniform. It is here that
Christians have invested the death and person of Jesus
with the meaning that they have learned in their own
experience.[13]

The explanations have centered on reconciliation, atonement, redemption, and salvation. They have ranged from
the ransom paid to the devil to the payment of the just
penalty to God for the infinite offense given by sin. They
have imputed to Jesus motives of obedience, love, compassion, and expiation. The explanations are important, of
course, not because they will ever decipher for us the
inner reality of God, or the psychology of Jesus, but because they express our understanding of our own role and
task in the work of Jesus yet to be completed, and because
they are attempts to understand concretely what that work
may be.

Today we are challenged by four configurations of Christian experience which particularly insistently call for a
soteriology—an explanation of the difference that Jesus
makes, what he died and lived for, and what it is concretely that is the focus and object of Christian hope and
Christian endeavor. These four configurations are in terms
of nonviolence, of challenge to every kind of domination
or oppression, of inner serenity and peace, and of freedom.
As they present themselves, they are often in conflict with
one another, or at least apparently so. Yet each of them has

the most respectable credentials in the tradition over the centuries.

The nonviolent configuration is something like the following.[14] Violence destroys both its object and its subject. But violence is pervasive in our relationships, social structures, codes of behavior, thinking. Violence is incompatible with love of God and love of neighbor. But we do not even recognize it in ourselves, and where we do recognize it any one person is quite helpless to make a stand against it. He could only be annihilated. But Jesus challenged violence and by refusing to retaliate when it was unleashed against him, unmasked it in the structures of his society and all society and in the hearts of men. By this he was the man of obedience, the great listener to God whose reign is not violence but self-gift through the freedom of man. By this Jesus reveals God and is revealed to us as divine. By this he participates in and expresses the very being of God, and is raised from death because this being is not destroyed by violence. We are engaged in the completion of the work of Jesus when by the light of his death we discern and unmask violence in ourselves and in others.

This model has antecedents in varieties of Christian pacifism from early days, in monasticism, in the Franciscan movement, and in the Anabaptist groups. It also has its saints, who would certainly pass on the basis of the two-fold scrutiny suggested earlier. It often appears to conflict with the model that is concerned with the challenge to every kind of domination and oppression. According to that model the world is in need of redemption because some men are so badly exploited by others, because the distribution of material and cultural resources is so unjust, and because so many men are not free to shape their own goals but are incorporated as objects into other men's history.[15] Change is almost impossible because those who are oppressed also have an oppressed consciousness and cannot make a breakthrough. Those who are the oppressors are blissfully unaware that there is anything wrong with the situation, and when confronted are so totally threatened in their interests and self-respect that it is almost impossible that there should be a breakthrough at any point. Yet Jesus challenged oppression and was willing to pay the ultimate price of total rejection and shameful death by terrible torture. It is in this that we recognize him as the revelation of the just God, it is in this that he is of the very being and stuff of God. God raised him up because it is not possible that this challenge made at this price and with this detachment and clarity can go unheard. In him the impossibility of the conversion for mankind is overcome and through the ages men are able to gather around him and find the freedom and the courage to turn their world around.

This model is certainly somewhat at variance with the model that sees Jesus as redeemer and Word of God because he has in himself and confers on others inner peace and serenity of mind. The focus here is not on anything that the individual owes to others but on himself and his psychological condition. It is a stance that seems to be very common among conventional churchgoers but equally common among dropouts from church and society. Redemption is needed because men are alienated from themselves, restless and not at peace within, not living authentically in accord with their own being but dissipating themselves in response to external pressures. Jesus appears as the man who is totally authentic, living and acting fearlessly without "hangups" and with utter spontaneity and sincerity. In the contemplative moments of his life he finds his balance for all situations. He "does his own thing" and even in his death he is wholly himself and is undisturbed. He is revealed to us as divine because he is not restless and because he can still the restlessness of those who come to him. In him we touch the stable, the timeless, the haven.

Introspective and self-focused as it is, this model nevertheless seems to have strong antecedents in Christian piety, in pastoral practice, and in some of the contemplative saints. It conflicts with the preceding models because it really assumes that the task is not the redemption of the world but of man's consciousness out of the world, and that the work of Jesus is furthered less by challenging injustice, violence and oppression, than by cultivating a detachment of spirit from it and helping the oppressed and sufferers to do likewise. Typically it is not unconcerned with others but it is unconcerned with their worldly fate, because it is only the inner consciousness that counts.

A more comprehensive model, perhaps, is that of freedom.[16] Mankind appears to be doomed to slavery of one kind or another; to be truly free is not just to have options before one, but rather to be wholly and comfortably committed to what complements and fulfills one's contingent being. To be truly free means to be neither slave nor master because the consciousness of both is warped. To be truly free is a task dependent on the freedom of others. Yet we live in a world of unfreedom, full of domination that breeds fear and self-defense and protects itself by dominating others. In such a world freedom appears as an impossible goal. The so-called freedom of "hanging loose," of protecting oneself by fair means and foul against possible inroads of others, appears to war against the freedom of man's destiny, because freedom for one can only be through the freedom of all the others, and because one only gives freedom to the others by exposing oneself to harm and annihilation.

Here Jesus appears as the very freedom of God erupting within the freedom of man. We see him as savior and see him as divine because in him the limits are broken and he is in the fullest sense free for others, free to offer freedom to others, free because of the inner freedom with which he is able to pay the price for that offering of freedom to others. And this freedom is the freedom of God himself —creative, salvific, and all-embracing.

These are some, but certainly not all the available models out of contemporary Christian life and spirituality which I submit must be taken seriously as basic to any contemporary Christology. They must of course be considered in the light of the whole tradition that went before and they must be scrutinized for the Christian credentials of those who present these models, but they are the stuff of the living tradition in our time. It is not in the philosophy or the biblical scholarship of our day that we can discover what difference Jesus makes for us. This we must discover from the patterns of Christian life and experience in the believing community as a whole, and the discovery will probably continue to leave us with paradoxical explanations of the uniqueness of Jesus.

NOTES

[1] In relation to the patristic era this is demonstrated, for example, by J. N. D. Kelly, *Early Christian Doctrines* (New York: Harper & Row, 1960), Chapter 14, though Kelly seems to see the developing and fluid character of the redemption theology as a misfortune. See also W. Pannenberg, *Jesus, God and Man* (Philadelphia: Westminster, 1968), Chapter 2; and P. Smulders, *The Fathers on Christology* (De Pere, Wisc.: St. Norbert Abbey Press, 1968).

In relation to mediaeval theology it is demonstrated, e.g., in *A Theology of Christ: Sources,* ed. Vincent Zamoyta (Milwaukee: Bruce, 1967), part three.

James W. Douglass, *The Non-Violent Cross* (New York: Macmillan, 1969), has exploited this distinction in an interesting and extremely fruitful way. See especially chapter three.

[2] See especially Bernard Lonergan, "The Dehellenization of Dogma," *Theological Studies,* 28 (1967), more particularly pp. 344–347.

[3] One who has treated it this way is Karl Rahner, e.g., in *Theological Investigations,* vol. III (Baltimore: Helicon, 1967), pp. 321–54. Also in *Christian in the Market-Place* (New York: Sheed & Ward, 1966), pp. 105–46.

[4] The Roman Catholic practice of such sanctions and canonizations has its close parallels, of course, in the other Christian communions.

[5] Most of the great contemporary theologians are or have been men of deep piety and frequently preachers, but it is noteworthy that they have two very distinct patterns as to sources and procedures of argumentation: one when they intend to do theology and another when they intend to edify.

[6] The term is, of course, that of John Henry Newman in his essay, "On Consulting the Faithful in Matters of Doctrine," which appeared in *The Rambler,* in 1859, and is reprinted in various collections of Newman's works.

[7] All theologizing has, of course, the spiritual base of the author but, no matter how totally he may live as a believer, this is but a poor substitute for the tradition, that is, the testimony of the Church as a whole.

[8] See the strong move in this direction by Bernard Lonergan in *Method in Theology* (New York: Herder and Herder, 1972), part two.

[9] The point is presented in detail by Piet Schoonenberg, *The Christ* (New York: Herder and Herder, 1971), especially pp. 56–58. Pannenberg's reflections on the matter are similar, *op. cit.,* pp. 291–294.

[10] These criteria seem to become explicit particularly in the selection of bishops.

[11] This would seem to be especially evident in the light of the Jewish prohibition of images of God because "man himself is the only image of God."

[12] The phrase became official, of course, in the Niceano-Constantino-politan creed that was to figure so prominently through the ages in the formation of Christian thinking concerning Jesus and his relation to the transcendent God. The other important images, such as Son of God, are not pursued in this paper.

[13] Apparently a matter of discomfort to some theologians, e.g., Pannenberg, *op. cit.*, pp. 47–52, yet obviously the necessary basis of any possible Christology.

[14] Given, for instance, in Douglass, *op. cit.*

[15] This model is implicit in J. B. Metz's "The Future in the Memory of Suffering" in *New Questions on God,* ed. J. B. Metz (New York: Herder and Herder, 1972).

It is also the standard model for Christology among the liberation theologians, e.g., Gustavo Gutierrez, *A Theology of Liberation* (New York: Orbis, 1973), part IV, section one.

[16] This model is set forth most strikingly in the works of Nicolai Berdyaev, e.g., *The Destiny of Man* (New York: Harper & Row, 1960). Even better, but much more difficult to obtain, is *Freedom and the Spirit* (London: Geoffrey Bles, 1935).

Jesus as the Horizon of Human Hope

ANDREW MALONEY

Does Jesus make a difference? The position of this essay is that indeed Jesus makes a difference. It is important, however, to have a viable conceptualization/verbalization of this affirmation in a language apt to mediate between faith's earliest witness in the New Testament and a truly contemporary consciousness. Theology, in other words, should be a vehicle that makes truly contemporary preaching possible in a language suitable for matters which we take with respectful seriousness.

Two points can be taken as established to the general satisfaction of all serious inquirers: Jesus was an historical character, not a pious fiction;[1] and it is impossible to write his biography although much can be known about him from the Gospels with reasonable assurance of historical correctness.[2] In reference to the second point: When we speak about history, we speak about Jesus. When we speak eschatologically, we speak about Jesus (the) Christ. Jesus was born, lived, preached and died. Jesus (the) Christ "lives" forever as the risen glorified Lord of history. It is, therefore, inappropriate and confusing to speak of *Christ's* birth, life, preaching and death. When Jesus was raised/ rose, he was raised/rose as (the) Christ and Lord. It is only out of the Christian faith commitment that Jesus is acknowledged as the Anointed. This controlled usage of

Jesus and (the) Christ is suggested in full knowledge of the fact that when the Gospel was received by Greek-speaking communities, the title Christ, which designated a function in Palestinian Christian communities, became as it were a proper name, and this from New Testament times.

Granted these two points, it could be affirmed that Jesus had a moral influence only. He would, thus, remain living in the same way as Socrates or Shakespeare does, that is, as a phenomenon of cultural history. Jesus would then be risen as Shakespeare is, that is, as one who, despite his death, remains effective in cultural history.[3] One might consign Jesus to the category genius, or hero, or mystic. With reservations, Nietzsche's point seems well made, "Renan, that buffoon *in psychologicis*, has introduced the two most inappropriate concepts possible into his explanation of the Jesus type: the concepts of *genius* and the concept of *hero*. . . . But if anything is un-evangelical it is the concept of the hero. . . . To make a hero of Jesus! And even more, what a misunderstanding of the word genius!"[4] Schoonenberg speaks to the same point, "Jesus is not a genius . . . neither is he primarily a hero . . . , but a holy man, 'the Holy One of God' (Mark 1, 24), 'the Holy and Righteous One' (Acts 3, 14). But he is not a holy man who is out of the ordinary: 'the Son of man came eating and drinking' (Matt. 11, 19), but one made holy by God's truth and trust, the one who sanctifies himself for others (John 17, 17), in a word: the holy one of love."[5] There would be, it seems, no commonly assignable category to include Socrates, Jesus and, let us say, Shakespeare.

As a variation of the morally influential interpretation, it could be affirmed that in Jesus' relationship to his disciples and in his death and resurrection, there occurred one Christ-event among other such events, as for example with Socrates or Martin Luther King, Jr. If, as we believe, Socrates and Martin Luther King "live" objectively to our consciousness, and not only by moral influence through the memory we have of them, it seems difficult to maintain that Jesus matters more than they. If the category Christ-event is not concrete-specific but abstract-generic, then it seems that no particular importance can be given to Jesus (the) Christ. His "rising" to be Christ is, then, one event among others, different perhaps in degree but not in kind. To us, however, it seems we would have no basis for affirming that Socrates or Martin Luther King live objectively to our consciousness did we not first, in faith, affirm that Jesus lives. It was uniquely in his case that death was shown to be overcome in him and for us. We do not think that "Christ-event" can be a category, except as primary analogue transcendent to its analogates. In *the* Christ-event we are confronted with the genuinely eschatological which cannot be assumed into a category inclusive of other events which, for us, remain historical. These historical events—the death of Socrates or of Martin Luther King—gain a new dimension when referred analogously to the Christ-event, but they do not become, for the Christian, genuinely eschatological.

In line with the immediately foregoing, it could be affirmed that the Christ-event in the risen Jesus is unique, once-and-for-all, but accessible to us only through the faith of the original communities of belief and that we need not concern ourselves about Jesus' historical life at all.[6] As far as history is concerned, it would suffice to know that Jesus did in fact die. Any search for his history would be un-necessary and, even if successful in some measure, would not be kerygma or proclamation, and hence would not call for the decision of faith. Faith is founded in the proclamation, not in history, except in the one case of Jesus' death. Whether, then, Jesus was brilliant or of mediocre talents, virgin-born or born of fruitful marriage, would not concern faith as such.

To us, however, it seems difficult to think that believers could be unconcerned about the history of that man whose death they believe to have been a victory over death. Was it not his life that led to his death and does not his history take on a new dimension of meaning for us from the perspective of his triumph over death in death? Psychologically, if not for other reasons, it seems impossible to say: Leave Jesus' history to the secular historians to make of it what they can; for us it matters only *that* he died and that his death was entry into "life" and calls us to life. It seems to us that if a Christian is to be integrally human in his belief, he must integrate belief with history, made available to him by accurate research. Faith seeks integration not only through understanding, but also in the dimensions of feeling and thirst for information. If this integration is not achieved, is it not likely that faith's rootage in history will be lost and the proclamation come to be seen as a beautiful myth among other myths which leave us unredeemed and our world unhealed?

The position taken in this essay has something in common with each of the preceding positions and comes close to the last mentioned, without identifying with it. We would affirm that, in Jesus' relationship to his disciples and in his death and resurrection, there occurred a unique, once-and-for-all decisive Christ-event, to which other Christ-events are analogous. This Christ-event is accessible to us only through the faith of the original and continuing communities of belief. That faith, however, relates inescapably to Jesus of Nazareth, whom it is important for us to know even historically, insofar as he is accessible to us as an historical character. The Gospels, in their own way, were interested in Jesus' history (witness the infancy Gospels in Mark and Matthew, their midrashic character notwithstanding). Our conviction is that the Christian theologian cannot sidestep the Gospels. He may criticize them, demythologize them, or even dissent from them insofar as they represent multiple and hence relativized theologies, but they are nevertheless primary data. They witness to and are formative of the historical Christian consciousness. They are our only significant documentary access to the Jesus to whom they relate and to the Christ and Lord whom the original believers profess. The Christ and Lord witnessed to in the Gospels is none other than the Jesus who lived and died among some of those who were still living when Paul was writing I Corinthians 15. The witness of the New Testament is to a consciousness that Jesus, despite his death, lives in a new and radically unaccountable fashion. What we find is not a profession of faith in a proposition, but the confident hope of believers founded in the conviction that Jesus has risen.

Much difficulty could be avoided if we were to remember that the consciousness of primitive Christian communities, both Palestinian and in a modified way Greek, is continuous with Judaic consciousness and its apocalyptic eschatology, which expressed itself in terms of the resurrection from the dead, not of the individual only but of the community of those who have departed life. Jesus is, in this light, understood to be the firstfruits of the risen from the dead, who will be joined by the righteous dead and the righteous living in the final consummation of history. In this connection, even granting that Greek dualism in anthropology may have already gained some access to the New Testament, it is important to notice that no anthropology is normative—neither Hebraeo-Judaic, nor Judaeo-Greek, nor Greek, nor existential. What is mandatory is to note that it is Jesus who lives as the Christ, not a revivified corpse, nor a disembodied soul. Whatever it is that constitutes the integrity of a human person continues on in Jesus (the) Christ. Thus, it is appropriate for us to mythicize this "continuing on" of Jesus in terms of a contemporarily recognizable anthropology. Here one can only point to the work of Gerhard von Rad in *Theology of the Old Testament*, of Willi Marxsen in *The Resurrection of Jesus of Nazareth*, and of others. The factual presence of a Greek anthropology as a minor counterpoint to Hebraeo-Judaic anthropology in the New Testament convinces us that no historically relativized interpretation of human existence is the unique vehicle of mythicization of the non-categorizable event in which Jesus became Christ and Lord.

Our approach to the question of Jesus' importance and indeed his uniqueness, has been much handicapped by a naïve materializing and historicizing of the Gospel evidences about the living Jesus and the "living" Jesus (the) Christ. We have forgotten that the living Jesus is magnified in function of the faith in the "living" Jesus (the) Christ and that the witness to the "living" Jesus (the) Christ is eschatological and not historical. We, some of us at least, have supposed that we must formulate an apologia for a re-invigorated corpse, for wondrous passage through solid objects, for ocular seeing of a risen body, and so on. In light of present knowledge, represented by Martin Dibelius and, more recently, by Jürgen Moltmann, ". . . something happened between Jesus' death and the faith of the early disciples." That something is non-categorizable, unique, without analogy to anything previously experienced. It could, and can continue to be expressed only in a mythic mode, in terms of appearances and empty tomb. A shift, then, to the consideration of the consciousness of the early believers, as the New Testament brings us to it, would give us another, less unbelievable theology. This consciousness is not unrelated to the Jesus of history, but it is not limited by this relationship either. "Something" has decisively formed it, either after or coincident with Jesus' death, to convince the early communities of belief that, no matter what the contrary appearances may seem to be, Jesus lives, and lives in a new and radically unaccountable way. As we also must do, they express the inexpressible and categorize the uncategorizable in mythic mode.

It is not unlikely that some might detect here a re-emergence of Docetism. Unlike the Docetists, for whose refutation the mythic account of Thomas' doubting was presumably formulated, and unlike the docetic aspects of devout Islamic belief, we must say with all the assurance that history permits that Jesus died as much as anyone can die, that his disciples saw him dead, and that at least the earliest disciples made no attempt to blink at his death. Whether he died for political (as seems probable) or for religious causes may be impossible to determine finally. That he died a malefactor's death, a deadly death, is as certain as any historical event can be. Whether three days later, or some short time later, or even coincident with his death (John)—it is of no essential concern which—his disciples became convinced that he "lives." For the disillusioned, disheartened disciples to have come to the confidence of his being "alive," *something* had to have happened. It stretches credibility beyond bounds to suppose that in the event, or shortly thereafter, they could have constructed a myth to assuage their disappointment (à la Reimarus). What happened was the "resurrection." The Resurrection is the thematization of an experience within the community of belief that the very dead Jesus lives. How he lives remains unknown. Faith, however, cannot but integrate itself and structures, over time, an account out of the materials it has in its possession, namely out of late Judaic apocalyptic eschatology. The how of Jesus' being alive—given the implied anthropology—comes to be expressed in terms of resurrection from the dead and of appearances to chosen witnesses. Hence arise the story of the empty tomb, the appearances as ocular seeing, and so on.

Did the disciples not, then, *see* Jesus? Respect for the evidences, primarily I Corinthians 15:1–11, demands an affirmative answer. Pannenberg's discussion of this, in his *Jesus—God and Man* commands attention.[7] Critical awareness demands of us that we qualify this seeing as an impingement of the genuinely eschatological on the consciousness of the witnesses, rather than as an ocular vision. They saw Jesus in the sense that they came to know, as an inescapable fact of faith-consciousness, that Jesus lives. They have an inner assurance, on a community basis, that Jesus lives despite his death. This assurance is founded in an experience undergone, but not produced by the consciousness of those who share it. The experience was ob-

jective to the consciousness in its cause, but of the eschatological dimension rather than of the historical. We might
say it was an experience of the *absolute* future which
relativizes all historical pasts, presents, and futures. In the
midst of those who believe, Jesus, as the presence of the
absolute future (God) towards whom history moves, in
other words as the Christ and Lord of history, relativizes
our present. Jesus enables us to become aware of the
negative aspects of our life, and calls us to their negation
while keeping us aware that the positive dimensions of our
existence, as they flow into the resultant vacuum, are themselves provisional, relative and, promissory before the un-
thinkable positive which God is as our absolute future.
Here, Moltmann's discussion of Christ as the horizon of
our present is of the greatest interest.[8] Our present is not
empty. It should not be devalued. It is, however, provisional, and its measure of fullness awakens in us hope for
the eschatological fullness of the absolute future.

To the objection raised by the skeptical that the earliest
disciples were suffering under an illusion, that they were
the unwitting victims of wish-fulfilment, one can only say
that such an objection is unanswerable *except within the
community of belief*. Love for the skeptic and respect for
his integrity demand that we give account of the faith we
profess. The works of believers, in this instance of the
earliest believers, vindicate the objective validity of their
faith. As evidenced in Acts, they strove to achieve true
human community, to share goods and wealth, to alleviate
all the needs of their fellows, to pass on to others the good
news that Jesus lives and hence we will live, that poverty
and misery are not final, that God is on the side of the oppressed, that true liberty is opening up for us, and so on.
That their achievement was not definitive from the be-

ginning does not invalidate the paradigm they present. They established wide-ranging confidence that, ultimately, life triumphs over death, freedom over slavery, justice over injustice, love over hate. Freedom, peace, justice, reconciliation, all the goods included in the metaphor "Kingdom of God," can be realized in our lives and in our history, not by way of any ultimate fulfilment but as the promise of that absolute future which history awaits in God who is present to it in Jesus (the) Christ.

It seems, therefore, that a mistake has been made in proclaiming Jesus as hero, as I had indicated in my previous remarks about Nietzsche and Schoonenberg. The hero Jesus is dead. The point is that although Jesus died, yet he "lives," no longer as Jesus merely but as Jesus whom, in living faith, we profess as Christ and Lord. The affirmation that Jesus is the Christ, that he is Lord, that he is the Holy One, and so on, is not of the historical order but of the eschatological. It is a judgment about the absolute future. Jesus' death was an entrance into another dimension, which we thematize in mythic mode as resurrection. Christianity is not Jesus-freaking. It is eschatological faith, rooted in historical event but not measured by it, unless negatively insofar as we fail to live up to the demands put upon us by Jesus (the) Christ in our own history.

In great part, Christians seem to have lost their zeal to preach the Gospel to all humankind. We have lost our missionary drive. The fact that we have no burning zeal to spread the good news is implicit acknowledgment that the Gospel has ceased to be good news for us. Unlike the earliest Christians, we no longer consider ourselves favored to be members of the household of the faith. We no longer consider ourselves privileged. Radically, this means that

Jesus (the) Christ has ceased to matter for us, ceased to be important to us, unless as the cipher for our individualist hopes to cheat death, while letting history go where it will. Perhaps this is attributable to our mistaken attempt to include Jesus (the) Christ in a category as hero, genius, mystic, revolutionary, hippie, or whatever. The world does not need another hero, genius, or mystic. It needs the impingement of its absolute future, to found its hope to energize its resources for good. Perhaps the only way that we shall regain our zeal for mission is to recover our conviction that faith matters to history, for the overcoming of history's negatives. We have been, understandably, disillusioned by the naïve attempt to draw a program for remedying history's negatives directly from the Gospel, as Johannes Metz has pointed out.[9] What we should look for in the Gospel is a certain perspective on these negatives, the gaining of an urgency for their overcoming and the confidence that they are, in fact, superable. Belief does not absolve us of the need to think, to research, to plan and to program. Rather, it mandates us to these tasks, and gives their undertaking a new dimension of value. We are not more knowledgeable as believers than the self-proclaimed unbeliever. We are the bearers of a consciously received mandate to share his burden and his work. If we fail to do this, we shall be the more accountable, having been given more.

As to whether Jesus matters and how, in the last analysis one must say that it is within the community of faith that he matters. He matters as the root and ground of present faith by his continuing presence, not morally but eschatologically, among the members of that community. He is not only in the midst of this community as visibly manifest in their love for each other, but in the integrity of his humanity. Ideally, he would be present to all as a true human community of love and service in conscious response to his call. This remains the eschatological hope, the ground of confidence in the absolute future. In the historical "meanwhile," we must strive to be the truly human community that we have been called to in (the) Christ, not declining into inwardness or mysticism in the privatizing and world-negating sense of the words decried by Bonhoeffer. The experience of present value within the community of belief would, one hopes, give us a new look at history. If our present experience of faith is negative, inhibiting, disempowering, then we shall not be able to see the liberating events that occur in our history in their relation to Jesus (the) Christ as the presence of the eschatological future in our historical midst.

The fact of the matter is, we think, that no Christology can be sustained without an ecclesiology. No ecclesiology, further, is sustainable without ecclesial experience. The present task is to build true communities of faith, responsive to the Gospel and hence responsible to history, open to the presence of him who lives. When we have built such communities of faith, then and then only will Jesus matter, and he will matter not as a dead but remembered hero, genius, or mystic. He will matter as the eschatological event whose continuing presence empowers us for the tasks of history. This he does through his Holy Spirit, in the love of the Father.

NOTES

[1] See Howard Clark Kee, *Jesus in History: An Approach to the Study of the Gospels* (New York: Harcourt, Brace and World, 1970), p. 60: ". . . these extrabiblical sources render extremely improbable the claim that Jesus is a pious fiction rather than an historical character."

[2] See Günther Bornkamm, *Jesus of Nazareth* (New York: Harper & Row, 1960), pp. 22–23: ". . . it cannot be seriously maintained that the Gospels and their tradition do not allow enquiry after the historical Jesus. Not only do they allow, they demand this effort. For whatever the opinions of historians on matters of detail, none can dispute that the tradition of the Gospels is itself very considerably concerned with the pre-Easter history of Jesus, different though this interest is from that of modern historical science. The Easter aspect in which the primitive Church views the history of Jesus must certainly not be forgotten for a moment; but not less the fact that it is precisely the history of Jesus before Good Friday and Easter which is seen in this aspect."

[3] Werner Harenberg, *Der Spiegel on the New Testament* (London: Macmillan, 1970), p. 235. The quotation, occurring in an interview with Bultmann under the title, "Is Jesus Risen as Goethe?" expresses this very well: "One can say that Jesus is risen as Goethe, if one views the person and work of Jesus as a phenomenon of cultural history. For the persons and works of great men remain effective in cultural history, and that goes also for Jesus. But if one understands Jesus as an eschatological phenomenon, and that means—according to Rom. 10:4: 'For Christ is the end of the law, that every one who has faith may be justified.'—as the end of world history insofar as its course is submitted to objectivizing observations, then his presence does not consist in his effect on cultural history, but it happens only in the moment of Christian proclamation and faith."

[4] Walter Kaufmann, ed., *Nietzsche: Philosopher, Psychologist, Antichrist* (New York: Vintage Books, 1968), pp. 339–340, cites the text from which this is abridged. Whether Nietzsche's preference for the word 'idiot' as suggested by Dostoievski's *The Idiot* is more justified than the words he is rejecting is a moot point. It, too, can have at best only qualified meaning in the world in which Jesus lives, and would seem to attempt to categorize Jesus (the) Christ, who is as such uncategorizable, unique.

[5] Piet Schoonenberg, *The Christ: A Study of the God-Man Relationship in the Whole of Creation and in Jesus Christ* (New York: Herder and Herder, 1971), p. 96.

[6] Rudolf Bultmann, *Jesus Christ and Mythology* (New York: Scribner, 1958), p. 80: ". . . what God has done in Jesus Christ is not an historical fact which is capable of proof." The eschatological event, which is what God has done in Jesus (the) Christ, can be grasped only by faith, not by objectifying world history.

[7] Wolfhart Pannenberg, *Jesus—God and Man* (Philadelphia: Westminster, 1968).

[8] Jürgen Moltmann, *Theology of Hope* (New York: Harper & Row, 1967).

[9] Johannes Metz, *Theology of the World* (New York: Herder and Herder, 1971).

Jesus as the Presence
of God in Our Moral Life

WILLIAM E. MAY

The significance of Jesus for our moral life or, better, our moral being, can be approached in many different ways. One could, for example, focus attention on the teaching of Jesus, in particular his call for conversion, his insistence that we put first the kingdom or reign of God, his challenge to love.[1] Or one could reflect on the meaning that Jesus has for our moral lives as Lord and redeemer, as sanctifier and justifier, as brother and servant.[2] Or one could, as I intend to do, seek to explore the significance of Jesus as the one who, as the light of the world, illumines human existence. In order to carry out this exploratory venture it will first be necessary to think about what it means to be a human being, for this is what we are and this what Jesus himself is, unless one regards him as did the Docetists —and to be a docetist is the perennial temptation of the Christian—as not really a man but simply as a God who temporarily took leave of heaven to walk the earth in the outward form of man. After this preliminary inquiry we can then try to see what is meant and what it means for us when we say that Jesus is the perfect man, and when we confess that this man Jesus is the personal, incarnate Word of the Father whose life he is and whose life he

113

offers us through himself and the Spirit that is his and his
Father's gift to us.

I

To be a human being is to be an animal. But a human
being, as René Dubos so beautifully puts it, is so *human*
an animal.[3] A human being is an animal, but an animal
with a difference. The difference can be expressed in different ways, but one major and critically important way
of putting this difference is to say that man, and man alone
of all animals, is a moral being. That man, and man alone,
is a moral being is illustrated in common speech. It is
meaningful, for instance, to speak about making human life
human. Yet to speak in this way seems paradoxical. We
would find it odd, indeed absurd, were someone to speak
of making bovine life bovine or canine life canine. A cow,
after all, is a cow and a dog is a dog. Yet it is not absurd
or meaningless to speak about making human life human.
Since it does make sense to speak in this fashion, it follows
that man is indeed a unique kind of animal, and it also
follows that the word "human" must be used in two quite
distinct ways when we talk about making human life
human. The second use of the term implies that a human
being is not totally human when he comes into existence.
Certainly no one who uses the term human in this second
sense wants to deny that all men are equally human beings
simply from the fact that they are all identifiably men, i.e.,
members of the same biological species. Yet he is affirming
that being human is not something factually given but is
rather a process, a growth, a matter of an individual human

being "becoming" human. To use the term in this second sense is to imply that there is a process of humanization; it is to imply that a human being has a destiny to which he is called and that he fulfills his being by his struggle to attain this destiny. In addition, to distinguish between two meanings of the term "human" is to affirm that not everything that man does and can do is really human. It is to distinguish between is and ought, between what men actually are and do, and what men ought to be and ought to do. It is, in short, to assert that man is a moral being, that human existence is a moral existence, that human history is a moral history.

But who is to tell us what being human in the second sense of this term is? Surely any one individual or group of individuals would be both foolish and arrogant to claim precise knowledge of what being human in this sense entails. Yet the search for the human in this sense is not meaningless or absurd. Man's strivings to find his identity and to discover meaning in life are not, as Sartre would have them, "useless passions." [4] Progress or growth in understanding the meaning of the human is possible, and it is possible because man as the inquiring, questioning being is the being who has within himself the preconditions making progress possible. To see what I mean here a passage from Bernard Lonergan is helpful, inasmuch as it sheds light on the dynamism that moves the human animal ever onward in his quest for meaning, truth, and responsible action. Lonergan writes:

Spontaneously we move from experiencing to the effort to understand; and this spontaneity is not unconscious or blind; on the contrary, it is constitutive of our conscious intelligence; just as the absence of the effort to understand is constitutive of stupidity. Spontaneously we move from understanding with its manifold and conflicting expressions to critical reflection; again, the spontaneity is not unconscious or blind; it is constitutive of our critical rationality, of the demand within us for sufficient reason, a demand that operates prior to any formulation of a principle of sufficient reason; and it is the neglect or absence of this demand that constitutes silliness. Spontaneously we move from judgments of fact or possibility to judgments of value and to the deliberateness of decision and commitment; and that spontaneity is not unconscious or blind; it constitutes us as conscientious, responsible persons, and its absence would leave us psychopaths.[5]

My purpose here is not to comment at length on this passage. Although many questions could be asked about it, its major thrust is clear. Human civilization, culture, and progress are possible because man is the being who asks questions, who inquires, who seeks to understand his experience, to test his understanding of experience for its truth, and to act responsibly in accord with a true understanding of himself and his world. And the dynamism that makes this movement from experience to responsible action possible, "far from being the product of cultural advance, is the condition of its possibility." [6]

The questions that man asks of his experience are of various sorts. Some are meaningful and can be given quick, final, definite yes-no answers: Is it raining outside? What is the chemical composition of salt? Others are meaningful, yet they can be answered only partially; the final, definitive answer can never be given simply because the questions reach out for or intend the unknown whole or totality of which our answers reveal only a part. Questions of this kind, called "transcendental" by Lonergan, move us from what we know to seek what we do not know yet. They are concerned with realities that are so rich in meaning, in intelligibility, that they are seemingly inexhaustible. They employ what Herbert McCabe calls "growing" words, words like love or loyalty or justice or human.[7]

Although these questions will never be given a final answer, this does not mean that they cannot be answered at all in a meaningfully true way. An example will help. I, for instance, am a father, standing in a certain relationship to my children. I do not believe that it is possible to give a definitive answer to the questions, "What is a father?" and "What is fathering?" But I do think that it is possible to tell with truth some things that this cannot mean: It cannot mean battering my children senseless if they disturb my watching a football game. Similarly, the final answer to the question concerning the meaning of the human cannot be given; still it is true to say, without being accused of being a wooden-headed legalist, that it cannot mean barbecuing neonates in order to test the psychological effect this has on their mothers, nor can it mean cheating the poor, nor stoning an adultress.

Our inquiring existence, moreover, is not solipsistic. As John Donne put it, "no man is an island." In our constant search for meaning and for truth we draw upon the collaborative efforts of our fellow men. Indeed, the world in which we live today is not, as Lonergan notes,[8] a world of pure, immediate experience. Rather it is a world where experience has been mediated to us by meaning, the meaning that our fathers and mothers, our grandparents, the whole human race before us, have discovered. We can question this meaning in the light of our own experiences, we can test it for its truth, but we do not start from scratch.

Man, the inquiring, social animal, differs from all other animals even in his corporate existence. For man is not merely gregarious; he is social, he lives in community, and his existence is a coexistence, his being is a being with. What ultimately makes his existence differ so markedly from that of other animals is his ability to speak. Man is the linguistic being. Why is this of such critical significance? Listen to these words of Herbert McCabe, for I think that they express this significance eloquently:

Man is the linguistic animal. When we say this we are not just pointing to a distinguishing characteristic of man. . . . Language does not only distinguish man from other animals, it distinguishes his animality from that of other animals. To be a man is to be an animal in a new sense, to be alive in a new sense. This means that even the activities which a man seems to share with other animals are transfigured by the fact that they are part of an animality that finally issues in language. Man does not just *add* speech on to such things as eating and sexual behavior; the fact that these latter occur in a linguistic context makes a difference to what they are.[9]

McCabe goes on to point out that world of animals is a world that is shaped or constituted in large measure by the animals' perception of it. This is true of man's world also, and like all other animals man seeks to share this world with his fellows through communication. But in man this communication reaches a new intensity, inasmuch as it becomes language. And, McCabe remarks,

It is important to see language not first of all in terms of the operation that is peculiar to it—the transfer of messages—but to see it as a mode of communication, a sharing of life. With the appearance of language we come to a . . . radical change, a change in which we do not merely see something new but have a new way of seeing, in which something is produced which could not be envisaged in the old terms and which changes our whole way of envisaging what has gone before . . . [it is] a new kind of life.[10]

The point McCabe is trying to put across may be clearer if we distinguish human language from the kind of communication or transferral of messages operative, for instance, in computer data bank retrieval systems. In these systems there is certainly communication in the sense that messages are transferred from one entity to another, that information is given and received, and that knowledge, in a sense, is accumulated. But the communication involved here is far different from the communication that takes place through human speech and language (and, it ought to be noted, men speak to one another not only by words but by their actions). Human language is not merely a matter of communicating a message; it is also a matter of communicating the messenger. Human language issues beyond communication in *communion*.

Communion among human beings is the ultimate purpose of human speech. This communion is achieved through understanding and love. Human beings are indeed interested in what is being said, but their basic interests are centered around who is saying it. Through our speech we reveal ourselves both to ourselves and to others, and vice versa. Through language we discover who we are and who we are meant to be. Our being as the human animal, the moral being, is a linguistic being. To be a man, to be a moral being, is to be a being who can communicate and share life.

II

At this point we are in a position to think about the meaning that Jesus has for our moral lives, for our being as the uniquely moral and linguistic animal. Jesus is, like us, a human being. But for us Christians he is the "perfect" human being. At one time in the history of the Christian Church, Jesus' perfection as man was thought to entail the most perfect kind of knowledge, power, and physical strength. Yet to say that Jesus, for instance, held the Copernican view of the universe or affirmed the Einsteinian theory of relativity seems absurd. The meaning of his perfection as man must be sought elsewhere. Perhaps the answer lies in his perfection as a linguistic being, as a speaker, as a word. In trying to think our way through on this matter we will be helped, I believe, by reflecting on some comments that Herbert McCabe has to make. He first of all distinguishes between the making of a perfect doorknob and the making of a perfect man. It is not as though God, after making a long series of defective men, finally came across the right formula and made the perfect man, Jesus, as a manufacturer might, after a succession of defective doorknobs, hit upon the right formula and come up with a perfect product. "The essential difference," McCabe writes,

is that each doorknob is a separate thing; it exists by itself and does not depend for its existence on its relationship to other doorknobs. The manufacture of doorknobs is just the making of one example after another, each one an isolated entity, whereas the making of men is the making of mankind; a man exists in his relationship to others. The perfect man, then, the being that man was meant to be, cannot be just an individual example of the human race; his perfection will consist in his setting up a new kind of relationship with the rest of mankind.[11]

He then continues:

To be a man is to be a centre of society, it is to be in communication with other men. . . . The imperfect man is the centre of a limited society, his capacity for communication is exhausted by this society and supported by a hostility to others. I mean that each of us finds himself, finds his identity, in the centre of our group of friends or fellow-countrymen or whatever. A social grouping is constituted by the overlapping social worlds of its members. Because they overlap there is a common world. This world is held together mainly by the common ties between its members but there is also the important external factor of exclusiveness. It is held together not only by love but also by fear; one of its bonds is a common hostility to what is alien. This is quite a common feature of other animal societies. . . . The claim that Jesus is perfectly human is the claim that his social world is coextensive with humanity, that he is open to all men and moreover open to all that is in man. It is not just that he would like to be or that he proposes this as an ideal . . . but that he actually is; the communication he offers is unmixed with domination or exclusiveness. So the coming of Jesus would not be just the coming of an individual specimen of the excellent or virtuous men, a figure whom we might try to imitate, but the coming of a new humanity, a new kind of community among men. For this reason we can compare the coming of Jesus to the coming of a new language; and indeed, John does this: Jesus is the word, the language of God which comes to be a language for man.[12]

McCabe, I am convinced, is on to something of tremendous importance for us in our effort to understand ourselves as moral beings and Jesus as the one who is the way, the truth, and the light. Men live in communities because their existence is inescapably a co-existence, their being a being with. In company with their fellows they seek to make for themselves the "good" life, to secure those real goods that, together, perfect them as men because they correspond to needs rooted in man's being. There is no need here to attempt to compile a catalog of these real goods perfective of human beings; among them we would surely count life itself, health, truth, friendship, justice. All these goods are real goods; each is a good *of* man, not *for* man; each is a good to be prized, not priced. These goods, which are constitutive of the *bonum humanum*, define aspects of our personality, of our being. In addition, and this is exceedingly important, they are common goods insofar as they are not my goods or your goods but rather human personal goods capable of being communicated to and shared by every human being.[13] Because they are real goods corresponding to needs existing in every human being just because he is human, they generate real rights; each human being has a claim on them, a right to them, precisely because he is a human being and because they are the realities that make a human being more human.[14]

We come to know these goods and to love them in the communities of which we are a part. And these goods that we love and the persons that we love, in whom they are incarnated, form the focus of our existence. And here is the rub! Our love for these goods and for those human beings with whom we share our lives and goods and hopes, while binding us together as a community wherein we find our own identity, keeps us apart from the stranger, the alien, the foreigner. We fear him; we are afraid that he and his comrades will rob us of the goods to which we have a right, forgetting that he and his have just as much a claim to these goods as we do. We hate him, we close our hearts to him and stop our ears so that we canont listen to his cries for help. We foolishly, though understandably, refuse to recognize his humanity and that of his comrades, deeming ourselves and our loved ones "more" or "better" men than they. We reject the notion that the goods we love are his goods too, and that the persons he loves and for whom he wills these goods are equally men as are the persons we love and for whom we will these goods. We reject his humanity because he is not one of us, because he is Jewish or Black or Oriental or poor or stupid or mean—or unborn. Yes, we love the *bonum humanum* and the men for whom the *bonum humanum* exists, only we are quite selective in judging whom we shall count as men.

What Jesus tells us, and tells us more by his being and his deeds than by his words, is that in rejecting the stranger or the alien because he is "other," we are really rejecting ourselves and our own identity, our own humanity. He is telling us that we are denying, by our deeds, our own drive to become men fully, for we can become men fully only if we accept our own humanity, as he did, and we can accept our own humanity only if we are ready to accept the humanity of every man we meet, whether he is friend or foe, fellow intellectual or stupid adolescent, avant-garde Catholic or devotee of Frank Morriss.

At this point it is instructive to note, I believe, that the direction in which we have been led by reflecting on McCabe's way of expressing the human perfection of Jesus seems to converge with lines developing from the thought of contemporary moral philosophers and theologians and the great systematic theologian, Karl Rahner. We will take the moral philosophers and theologians first. Despite differences, such moralists as Germain Grisez, Josef Fuchs, Bruno Schüller, and Richard McCormick agree that the *bonum humanum* is, as indicated above, pluriform, i.e., composed of individual real goods that together go to comprise the good of man. They regard these real goods (e.g., life, health, justice) as "nonmoral" or "premoral," and their destruction brings about what can be called "nonmoral" or "premoral" evil or *evil* as distinguished from *wickedness*. Morality or, better, our identity as moral beings, enters when we consider our attitudes toward these premoral goods and our pursuit of them. To regard them as ours, and ours alone, is wicked; to pursue them and, in the pursuit, to destroy them in others is wicked, because this indicates that we are willing to hate them in others and that we are open to their realization only in ourselves.[15] To look on these goods in this way and to seek them in this way means, ultimately, that we are simply not ready to grant that other men have the same claim to them as we do, and they have this claim precisely because these goods are truly perfective of human beings, are indeed personal goods of every human being. What these moralists are saying, in other words, is that wickedness stems from our heart, from the core of our being. It springs from a heart that is hardened against the claims of other men, that refuses to recognize them as being men on the same footing as ourselves.

Rahner's approach puts the focus somewhat differently, but his thought seems to converge with that of McCabe and the moralists previously noted. Rahner's point is that a full acceptance of our own humanity is possible only if we accept the humanity of others, and that acceptance of the humanity of our fellow men is implicitly an acceptance of Christ and of the God who sent him to us.[16] And, it must also be noted, the capacity to accept fully our own humanity is a capacity that is ours because there is a God who loves us and has become one with us and summons us to his own life.[17]

Perhaps the matter could be put this way. As the one who opens our eyes to a new mode of communication, Jesus is telling us that we are, as linguistic and moral beings, *responsive* beings. Human communication through language implies that human existence is meant to be a dialogue, not a monologue. In a dialogue one person addresses another, and the other replies or responds. Our being as moral beings, in other words, is dialogical, and this means, literally, *through a word*. If we now look on human existence in this way and reflect on this existence as Christians, i.e., as those who believe that Jesus is the Father's Word to men, we will soon see that all men are, in a true sense, "words" addressed to other men by their loving Father. We are the created words that the Uncreated Word became. To be a man, to be a human being, to be a moral being, then, is to be that being whom "God himself," as Karl Rahner puts it, "becomes (though remaining God) when he exteriorizes himself into the dimension of what is other than himself, the non-divine." [18] To be a man, then, is to be that being that "ensues when God's self-utterance, his Word, is given out lovingly into the void of god-less nothing." [19] Man, in short, is the "code-word" for God, and the living God of history, the God who "othered" himself in Jesus of Nazareth, is to be discovered "precisely where we are, and can only be found there." [20] Put in another way, we can say that man's existence, as disclosed to us in Jesus, is the ultimate reason why there is the divine command not to make graven images. The reason is simply that God has already made his image, and this image is man, who is his living icon, an icon that God himself became in Jesus.

In our struggle to find ourselves, to discover our identity, to fulfill our destiny, moreover, we need help. Our moral lives are not lived in some kind of vacuum, and to do what we know to be the right thing, the human thing, we need help and support. This point is brought home graphically to us by a passage in St. Paul's letter to the Romans, where he writes: "I do not understand my own actions. For I do not do what I want, but I do the very thing I hate. . . . I can will what is right, but I cannot do it. For I do not do the good I want, but the evil I do not want is what I do" (7:15–19).

Something paradoxical, indeed something indicative of the depths of man's existence, is at stake here. The paradox can only make sense if we admit that there are operative in human existence factors that John Macquarrie, in a magnificently perceptive passage, has called disabling or crippling and enabling or supportive factors.[21] We do not pull ourselves up by our own bootstraps, as it were. We do not live as isolated entities, in a vacuum, but in a world wherein we find both support and non-support. We live, in short, in a world of tension between sin (the disabling factors) and grace (the enabling factors).

We live, it must be acknowledged, in a world that has been wounded by sin, by man's failure to respond in trust and love to the words uttered to him by the Father, and uttered to him in the person of his fellow men. Sin is a reality, and its reality has important repercussions on our struggle to do what we know to be right or human. But, as Macquarrie reminds us,[22] the world in which we live is a world in which grace is also operative and is, indeed, prior to sin. As Christians we know that the God we love is an Emmanuel, a God who is, as Karl Barth has put it, "neither next to man nor above him, but with him, by him, and most important, for him." [23] Our God is the God who became one of us in Jesus. And this God is with us now, for Jesus is, and he is still man. Although many, infected by a docetist mentality, imagine that Jesus, after being raised from the dead, went back to being God again, our faith is that this man Jesus is still one of us, is still man, is the first-fruits of the dead. As man he is still with us, present to us in our struggle to make sense of our lives, in our efforts to discover our identity. He is with us even if we refuse to recognize him, and he offers himself to us personally in the *zoa logika*, the created words, the *eikones theou* whom we meet in our daily lives, and with whom we collaborate in our efforts to build the human. We know this because he told us that in giving a cup of water to a stranger we are giving it to him. We know this because with Paul we believe that nothing, "neither angels nor principalities, neither the present nor the future, nor powers, neither height nor depth nor any other creature, will be able to separate us from the love of God that comes to us in Christ Jesus our Lord" (Rom. 8:35–39).

NOTES

[1] This is the approach taken by, among others, Charles E. Curran in his "The Central Message of Jesus: Conversion" in *A New Look at Christian Morality* (Notre Dame, Ind.: Fides, 1968).

[2] For a scholarly study of these approaches to Jesus and our moral lives, see James Gustafson, *Christ and Our Moral Life* (New York: Harper & Row, 1968).

[3] René Dubos, *So Human an Animal* (New York: Random House, 1969).

[4] Jean-Paul Sartre, *Being and Nothingness*, trans. Hazel Barnes (New York: Philosophical Library, 1956), p. 615.

[5] Bernard J. F. Lonergan, *Method in Theology* (New York: Herder & Herder, 1972), p. 18.

[6] *Ibid.*, p. 11.

[7] Herbert McCabe, *What Is Ethics All About?* (Washington: Corpus, 1969), pp. 18–19.

[8] Lonergan, *op. cit.*, pp. 20–25.

[9] McCabe, *op. cit.*, p. 68.

[10] *Ibid.*, pp. 74–75.

[11] *Ibid.*, pp. 127–128.

[12] *Ibid.*, pp. 128–129.

[13] On this see Jacques Maritan, *The Person and the Common Good* (New York: Scribners, 1948).

[14] See Mortimer Adler, *The Time of Our Lives* (New York: Holt, Rinehart and Winston, 1971), chapter 6.

[15] See Germain Grisez, *Abortion: The Myths, the Realities, and the Arguments* (New York: Corpus, 1970), p. 312 ff. On the views of Schüller and Fuchs, see Richard McCormick, "Notes on Moral Theology," *Theological Studies* 32 (1972), pp. 68–72.

[16] Karl Rahner, "Jesus Christ, IV. History of Dogma and Theology," in *Sacramentum Mundi* 3, 194. (New York: Herder and Herder, 1969).

[17] *Ibid.*

[18] Rahner, "On the Theology of the Incarnation," in *Theological Investigations*, vol. 4 (Baltimore: Helicon, 1966), p. 113.

[19] *Ibid.*, p. 116.

[20] *Ibid.*

[21] John Macquarrie, *Three Issues in Ethics* (New York: Harper & Row, 1970), pp. 119–125.

[22] *Ibid.*, p. 122.

[23] Karl Barth, *Introduction to Evangelical Theology* (New York: Holt, Rinehart and Winston, 1963), p. 11.

The Divine Acceptance of Man's Holy and Sinful History

ROBERT KRESS

Does Jesus make a difference? In many respects he does not, for he was not a political reformer, a charismatic catalyst for social change, a scholarly or creative or any other kind of genius. Although fully Jewish (Gal. 4:4), he was not simply another Pharisee.[1] He was a religious leader and teacher and thus honored with the title Rabbi (Mt. 23:7–8). Hence the opening question can be directed to his teaching, especially insofar as this is often a clarification of his religious leadership actions. Did Jesus teach anything that really made a difference?

The decisive difference in his teaching is his interpretation and clarification, both doctrinal and personal, of God's holiness.[2] The holiness of God is his very being, is revealed in Jesus precisely in that he is and is recognized as the "friend of sinners" (Mt. 11:19; Lk. 7:34). Already in the Old Testament there is a clear progression in the understanding of God's holiness, as especially the prophet Isaiah illustrates. Overwhelming and awesome in the early chapters, this divine holiness is later understood to be compassion and consolation (compare Is. 7 with Is. II and III). The Roman liturgy had recognized this very well in the prayer prescribed for the priest before the proclamation of the Gospel: The burning coal of Isaiah has become the *gratia miseratione* for the priest. Hosea clearly understands that the holiness of Yahweh does not reject the fallen woman, his spouse Israel. Rather, he seeks her out and through his loving embrace heals and gives her new being, as the new names in the story indicate. Jeremiah and Ezekiel are vivid testimonies that it is precisely the divine holiness of God that is neither destroyed nor put off by the sinner. In fact, it is precisely the holy being of God that makes it impossible for him to desert his fallen bride (Ezek. 36:5, 22).

Against this Old Testament background the disputes of Jesus with his contemporaries can be seen to be more than mere prolepsis of later conciliar Christological controversies. The question is of course about the person of Jesus, especially about his authority. However, the dispute is not only about the formal, doctrinal authority of Jesus, but also the material content of his doctrines. Indeed, it is not illegitimate to suggest that the dispute over his formal authority arose from the content of his teaching, both word and deed.

The decisive distinction between Jesus and other current interpretations of the covenant was not only his claim to be able to forgive sin (Mk. 2:1–12), but his willingness to be with sinners, even to eat with them (Mt. 2:15–17). It is in this latter difference that the difference that Jesus makes is to be sought. Jesus and his opponents have much in common—the Law, the prophets, the Temple, wisdom. What decisively separates them in their interpretation of their heritage is the strong separatism of the Pharisees, Sadducees, Essenes, and, in a different way, the Zealots.[3] However else these sectarians might have differed

among themselves, and however much good they might
have accomplished, they are one and reprobate in their refusal to acknowledge that it is precisely the holiness of
God that does not reject, but seeks out the sinner. The
mercy parables of Luke 15 as well as Jesus' claims to be
the good shepherd highlight the fact that Jesus is the only
valid interpreter and interpretation of the Promise given
to Abraham, the Law given to Moses, and the Kingdom
given to David. Only Jesus is the gate to abundant life—
all conflicting interpreters are thieves and brigands who
kill and destroy (Jn. 10:1–10).[4] How different the Jesus
interpretation of the covenant is from other conflicting
contemporary ones is illustrated by Simon the Pharisee
(Lk. 7:47) and the scribes and Pharisees who caught the
woman in adultery (Jn. 8:1–11). That such actions are not
merely passing fancies or symbolic gestures on the part of
Jesus is indicated by his doctrine of perfection: To be perfect is to be compassionate even to sinners, as God is.[5]
Jesus carries this understanding of God's holiness to its
human and divine ultimate on the cross where his reaction
to the sin of his rejection is precisely not to reject his
rejectors, but to pray, "Father, forgive them" (Lk. 23:34).

Thus is fulfilled that newness of the covenant which
Jesus had come to proclaim and be. Anticipated and hoped
for in the Old Testament (Ezek. 36; Jer. 31), the new
covenant in the blood of Jesus is entered at the Last
Supper of the Holy One of God (Mk. 1:24) with sinners.
It is indeed for the many, that is, for the remission of sin,
the forgiveness of sinners.[6] As befits Jesus, the Son of the
living God (Jn. 19:7; Lk. 21:38), this outpoured blood does
not terminate in death, but in another Paraclete (Jn.
14:16, 26), the power of God (Lk. 24:49) who is the

forgiveness of sins (Jn. 20:19; Lk. 20:19, 24:47; and Acts 1:8),[7] and in missionary witnesses who proclaim and minister the forgiveness of sins in the name of Jesus Christ (Acts 2:38).

At this point we begin to speak of the Church. It is the enspirited disciples (believers, followers) of Jesus. That is, it is the continuing Jesus interpretation of the "Old" Covenant. It is the memory of Jesus, the tradition of Jesus. It is thus the "New" Covenant. We must avoid thinking of the Old, but most especially the New Covenant as a sort of third thing between God and the people. A text from the Epistle to the Hebrews is decisive (8:7–8). The covenant is the people in their relationship with Yahweh: Emphasis is on this general interiority as well as the immediacy of the people's knowledge of God and the forgiveness of sins (8:9–12).

Like its founder and source, this Church of the New Covenant is also the friend of sinners. It is and must stand as the memory of him who came "at the end of the last age, to do away with sin sacrificing himself" (Heb. 9:26). As Jesus, the Church is the refuge of sinners.[8] Unlike its sinless source (Jn. 8:46; Heb. 4:15; 2 Cor. 5:21), however, the Church is not without sinners and hence not without sin. But it need not be sinless since the whole history of salvation from Adam to Jesus has shown that God's holiness is able to live and be with sin and sinners. Hence the holiness of the Church as the memory of the presence of the Holy One of God among men does not require the absence of sinners and sin in it. It is not God, but the sacramental presence of God among sinners. Founded in sinners, it has always been composed of sinners. From the very beginning provision had been made for this Holy Church of sinners

(Mt. 18:18; Jn. 20:19). That there was no golden age[9] (in spite of Acts 2:42–47) is amply testified by those very same Acts of the Apostles, as well as all the epistles (not least to the Corinthians, who are so often so unduly touted as the model or ideal church). Already the book of Revelation can find only two churches beyond reprimand, while three are mediocre at best, and two are reprobate. The symbolic character of the number seven (fullness, universality) may not be overlooked. This is not a random selection of seven individual churches. It is the Church that is holy and sinful.

The Church, holy-sinful from its inception, must mediate its history as the tension and struggle between holiness and sinfulness in itself. Practically this struggle has frequently taken the form of attempts to exclude sinners from the Church. In fact, the earliest doctrinal tendency (originally within the Church) to evoke rejection by episcopal synods was Montanism.[10] Tertullian has the oracle speak: "The Church can forgive sins, but I will not do so, lest others also commit sin" (*De Pudicitia*, 21). The end result of such a theology would be the destruction of the Church, as the like-minded Novatian heresy showed shortly thereafter. The earliest deviant doctrines were generally rigorist, elitist, and separatist. Their paradigm was Novatianism. After the Decian persecution (249–251), the question of the forgiveness and re-admission of the *lapsi* was debated. Originally lenient, Novatian, frustrated in his bid to become pope, adopted a rigorist attitude. This rigorism increased and in 251 the episcopal synod of Rome condemned his teaching and expelled his followers from the Church. It is noteworthy that the first anti-pope arose in opposition to a Church of sinners and forgiveness. That such rigorism is inherently destructive of the Church is forcefully illustrated by a Novatian text from Spain: "After Baptism there is no penance anymore; the Church cannot forgive any mortal sin and she destroys herself when she admits sinners." The followers of Novatian were eventually named "the pure people" (*cathari*; Eusebius' *History of the Church* VI, 3, 11) and survived in small sects until the seventh century. The opposition to these sectarian and elitist views enabled the church of the bishops to be and become the great church of compassion for sinners, as its founder had wished.[11]

St. Augustine, in spite of the *massa damnata*, prefers *catholica* (252 times) as the best designation of the Church. The Middle Ages are famous for reform movements, orthodox and not. In all the deviant forms there is a remarkable elitist and purist separatism. Their "Church" excludes the weak and failing and is thereby reduced to an inconsiderable sect. Hus and Wyclif are not at all able to retain the sinner in the Church. In fact, soon only the predestined are the Church.[12]

From Luther came the great theological slogan, "simul justus et peccator." But Protestantism in general has by no means remained true to this insight. In the Congregational and Free Church traditions it has been relinquished altogether. Hans Urs von Balthasar points out that not only is the slogan acceptable to Roman Catholicism, but that only there does it enjoy its full meaning.[13] In this same line of thought, various authors have pointed out that Roman Catholic and Protestant ecclesiologies have pursued different paths: Protestantism that of purity (holiness) and Catholicism that of universality and fullness.[14]

For all of its vacillations,[15] Catholicism has been much more expansive and all-embracing, even of the sinner.

Thus the Council of Trent, at pains to retain the sinner within the Church, insisted on the *fidelis peccator* (DS 1537). A recent and as yet unpublished doctoral dissertation at the University of Innsbruck established that the Tridentine *actus judicialis* of the confessor (DS 1684, 1709) does not refer so much to the deliberative function of the priest as judge, but rather to his sacramental power to establish the penitent in the state of forgiveness proclaimed in the absolution.[16] This would certainly be in the spirit of Jesus, who was most concerned not with judicial process but with precisely the forgiveness of sin.

Not all these insights were preserved after Trent. In fact, the theological manuals written in the century before Vatican II are generally quite hesitant and reluctant about the sinner in the Church. The general strategy is little more than a ploy—the distinction between the holy Church and sinful members. The sinner remains within the Church theoretically, but practically he is relegated to the margin or periphery. This "lateral" status of the sinner is in sharp contrast to Vatican II, which speaks of "the Church embracing sinners in her bosom" (constitution on the Church, n. 8). Notice that it does not say "to" but "in." Thus is indicated an intense perichoresis of even the sinful member and the Church.[17] Of course, by this I wish by no means to assert equality of Church inhesion for both saint and sinner.

The same text also speaks of the Church "at the same time holy and always in need of being purified." The similarity of this statement with the Lutheran *simul justus*

is obvious. But the Council itself was not quite able to pre-
dicate sinful of the holy Church, as one of Pope Paul's
interventions in the ecumenism document shows (n. 3).
The words "in its members" were added to the original
text, which had read "During its pilgrimage on earth this
People, though still (intervention) liable to sin. . . ." I
have shown elsewhere that this papal intervention is not a
diriment impediment to the concept of the "sinful holy
Church." What was regarded as a theological dispute
within Catholicism was not to be given a conciliar resolution.[18] Hence it is theologically legitimate to speak of the
sinful holy Church, and to draw practical conclusions
therefrom.

I am not unaware that this essay can be accused of imbalance in favor of the scriptural and historical portions.
However, in regard to the present subject I have noticed
that frequently what is well known "factually" is not well
understood "meaningfully." Hence I have chosen to emphasize the fundamental understanding that Jesus reveals
God's being-holiness as the friend of sinner. This is normative for an understanding of the Church. I shall now suggest how such an approach reveals the specific difference
that Jesus makes and simultaneously makes both Jesus and
his Church relevant to modern man.

THEOLOGY: This concept does not seek the real Jesus
where he cannot be found, and constantly recalls the
Church to its own most proper nature and mission. It
allows God to be God and grants his holiness the primacy,
for the formula "sinful holy Church" allows sin only an
adjectival dignity—the substantive is the "holy Church."

It promotes an adequate Judaeo-Christian ontology in which being is clearly understood to be originally given (creation) and subsequently forgiven (redemption) and salvation consists of both of these: from nothingness in the creation and from sin-death in the redemption. Furthermore, such a formula would prevent the dislocation of the Church in only one of its dimensions—especially the institutional, sacramental, or hierarchical. It is a helpful means of assuring continuing awareness that the Church is the people.

PSYCHO-THEOLOGY: Such an ecclesiology allows finite contingent man to be such, for it fully accepts the reality of failure without glorifying it (mystique of sin), or explaining it away (situation ethics), or diminishing human dignity by denying man the possibility of sin (secular humanism, ethical culture, and similar dwarf anthropologies).[19]

SOTERIOLOGY: It allows the dreadful (Rom. 7:24) reality of man's failure and sin, but does not accord it the last word. Sin is thus de-absolutized and relativized [20] for even sin points to the holiness of the Church and God which is the ultimate. Thus the ultimate sin-induced failure, death, is not really ultimate for even this last enemy of death is being destroyed (1 Cor. 15:26). How could it be otherwise? Where sin and its companion death abounded, the life-holiness-being of God in Christ has abounded even more (Rom. 5:12–21).

SPIRITUALITY: Practically it should help us to relax and quit worrying about sins, ours and others, and get on

with Jesus' business of proclaiming the reign and kingdom of God in all the cities of the world (cf. Lk. 4:43).
Unlike Luther, who at one time had to say "I could not but
blanch . . . when I even heard the name of Christ . . .
whom I took to be a stern and angry Judge" (Werke
Weimarer Ausgabe, 1883, XL, I p. 298), and in contrast
to those "silly women who are obsessed with their sins and
follow one craze after another in the attempt to educate
themselves, but can never come to a knowledge of the
truth" (2 Tim. 3:6), we know "the wisdom that leads to
salvation (is) through faith in Christ Jesus" (2 Tim. 3:15),
the friend of sinners. His everlasting revelation of the
divine—"Neither do I condemn thee" and "Father, forgive
them"—is most strikingly preserved and realized in his
Church, which humbly confesses that it is indeed his sinful
church, but simultaneously rejoices that it is also his in-
vincibly holy Church.[21]

NOTES

[1] That Jesus was not a social or political revolutionary has been amply
shown by Oscar Cullmann, *Jesus and the Revolutionaries* (New York:
Harper and Row, 1970). Whether John T. Pawlikowski, "On Renewing
the Revolution of the Pharisees," *Cross Currents*, XX (Fall, 1970), pp.
414–34, sufficiently acknowledges the severe disagreement of Jesus with
his contemporary Pharisees is moot. The article is most valuable for its
rehabilitation of the Pharisees, who have received a bad press from the
Gospels on. Of course, this is also understandable since the early Church
was most interested not in what it had in common with the Pharisees
and the Jews, but in its specific difference within the common heritage.
It is also important to bury once and for all the Romantics' mischief of
picturing Jesus as utterly simple and naive. W. F. Albright has provided
some astringent observations on the theology of Jesus as the clown and
fool in his Anchor Bible commentary on *Matthew* (Garden City: Doubleday, 1971), *passim*, but especially p. clxxxv.

[2] For the importance of a correct concept of God's holiness for ecclesiology, see R. Latourelle, *Christ and the Church* (Staten Island: Alba House, 1972), pp. 217–227; for the Church in the modern world, see H. Muhlen, "Sakralität und Amt zu Beginn einer neuen Epoche," *Catholica* 1 (1972), pp. 69–83.

[3] It is possible that some of the parables urging patience are directed against the Zealots, who had their own version of purity and rejection of sinners within the community. See J. Jeremias, *The Parables of Jesus,* rev. ed. (New York: Scribner, 1963), p. 152. On the separatism of the Pharisees, even their name, *ibid.,* pp. 223–227. W. F. Albright also points out the differences between Jesus and his contemporaries insofar as the latter tended to be separatists and sectarians, *op. cit.,* pp. 125, 224, 296, 323.

[4] See R. Schnackenburg, *Das Johannesevangelium. II Teil Herders theologische Kommentar Zum Neuen Testament,* IV, 2 (Freiburg: Herder, 1971). "Indem Jesus, der Hirt, in die Funktion der Tür eingewiesen wird, zerbricht an ihm jeder illegitime Offenbarungs—, Führungs—, und Heilsbringeranspruch" (p. 364). "Der Anspruch Jesu richtet sich nicht nur gegen das Judentum, sondern hat eine universale, absolute Geltung" (p. 365).

[5] Thus, when J. Ratzinger wishes to illustrate the difference between the god of the philosophers and the God of Jesus, he precisely chooses Luke 15, which can in no way be construed as a random choice. See *Introduction to Christianity* (New York: Herder and Herder, 1970), p. 100. W. F. Albright translates Mt. 5: 48 "Be true, just as your heavenly Father is true." His commentary indicates that true being is merciful being. "A rabbinic commentary (TB, Shabbath 133b), quoting a first-century A.D. authority, paraphrases this as: 'Be like him. As he is gracious and merciful, so be you gracious and merciful.' The Greek word *teleios* in the context does not refer to moral perfection, but truth, sincerity (cf. Deut. xviii, 13). It does not here have the later Greek meaning of being 'totally free of imperfection,' which is the meaning found in both the King James and Revised Standard Version." *Op. cit.,* pp. 71 f. Cf. p. 232.

[6] Whether for the many, for us, for sinners, for the forgiveness of sins or sinners, this insight belongs to the earliest understanding of Christ, his person, and mission, especially his death-resurrection. See K. Lehmann, *Auferweckt am dritten Tag nach der Schrift,* 2nd rev. ed., (Freiburg: Herder, 1969), pp. 87–157, 247–57.

[7] As the Roman liturgy for Whittuesday so trenchantly affirms: "Mentes nostras, quaesumus, Domine, Spiritus Sanctus divinis reparent sacramentis: quia ipse est remissio omnium peccatorum" (Postcommunion prayer).

[8] I have tried to develop this theme both theoretically and practically in two books which will be published in the near future under the titles *Sinner at the Center* and *Sinful Holy Church*. In the meantime I refer the reader to an article in which I show that even though this title, "Refuge of Sinners," has been largely restricted to Mary, the recent Mariological emphases have been anything but conducive to such an understanding. R. Kress, "Mariology and the Christian's Self-Concept," *Review for Religious*, 31 (May 1972), pp. 414–420.

[9] See B. Schneider, "Bemerkungen zur Kritik an der Kirche," in H. Vorgrimler *Gott in Welt Festgabe Karl Rahner* (Freiburg: Herder, 1964), II, p. 249.

[10] See J. Lebreton and J. Zeiller, *Heresy and Orthodoxy* (New York: Collier, 1962), p. 68.

[11] "So this first dispute (over the discipline of Penance) was not in any way a battle between Rome and Carthage; it was the expression once again of two theories of the Church. For Novatian the Church was a small group of the spiritually-minded, in inevitable conflict with the earthly city: a Church of prophets and martyrs. On the other side was the bishops' view; for them the Church was a people which must gather together all men, and must therefore take account of the different levels implied by the arrival of a great many people within the Church. There was a place for an elite of spiritually-minded members; monasticism would satisfy their needs, but there was also room for the immense crowd of ordinary Christians. In this there was no relaxing of the Gospel's demands; this attitude was the traditional attitude of the Church. Cyprian and Cornelius were its great witnesses in the third century and thus prepared the way for the unfolding of the Constantinian Church, whereas the sect of 'pure people', as Eusebius calls the disciples of Novatian (*HE*, VI, 3, 11), gradually withered away." Jean Danielou and Henri Marrou, *The First Six Hundred Years*, vol. 1 of *The Christian Centuries*, ed. Louis Rogier (New York: McGraw-Hill, 1964), p. 199. "It is the lasting merit of the Church of the third century in the often intense struggles for a right understanding of Christian penance in the face of the rigorism that kept flaring up again and again, to have defended the spirit of compassionate understanding for the sinner which the founder of the Church preached, and yet to have prevented the incursion of lax tendencies into Christian penitential discipline." Karl Baus, *From the Apostolic Community to Constantine*, vol. I of *Handbook of Church History*, eds. Hubert Jedin and John Dolan (London: Burns & Oates, 1965), p. 345.

[12] Among the opinions attributed to Hus and rejected by the Council of Constance, the first clearly restricts the holy and one Church to the

totality of the predestined (DS 627, 633). The same council also rejects the idea that the grace of predestination is the bond of unity within the Church and between the Church and Christ its head (DS 629, 631, 647). As might be expected, the Council Fathers did not look kindly on John Wyclif's contention that the (Roman) Church was "the synagogue of Satan" (DS 617). The undoing of such reformers was their impatience and inability to accept the fact that God does indeed tolerate the sinner, patiently, as the parables of the wheat and tares as well as of the prodigal son (which should be named the parable of the generous father) insist.

[13] Hans Urs von Balthasar, *Karl Barth*, 2nd edition (Köln: Jakob Hegner, 1962), pp. 378–386.

[14] See Yves Congar, *La Sainte Eglise* (Paris: Cerf, 1963), "M Jean Guitton a pu caracteriser le catholicisme comme recherche de la pléntitude, et le protestantisme comme volonté de pureté. La suggestion est assez éclairante. J. Hessen en a fait une analogue" (p. 152). The theme is developed somewhat by Congar in *Vraie et fausse réforme dans l'Eglise*, rev. ed., (Paris, Cerf, 1968), pp. 278–300.

[15] I think here of the practice of excommunication (whether it is really excommunication or not; cf. A. Gommenginger, "Bedeutet die Exkommunikation Verlust der Kirchengliedschaft?" *Zeitschrift für katholische Theologie*, 73 (1951), pp. 1–71). J. Ratzinger has pointed out the serious deterioration caused in the understanding of the Church by the misuse of excommunication in the Middle Ages, especially by the popes: "faktisch hat die Diskreditierung der Communio duch die Politisierung der Exkommunicatio und so die Sprengung des altkirchlichen Modells heraufgeführt. Die konkrete Kirche ist nun nur noch Institution und als solche, geistlich betrachtet prinzipiell zur quantité négligeable geworden." J. Ratzinger, "Opfer, Sakrament und Priestertum in der Entwicklung der Kirche," *Catholica*, 26 (1972), p. 117.

[16] See Franz Gräf, *Die Lehre vom richterlichen Charakter des Bussakraments, insbesondere der Absolution auf dem Konzie von Tuent* (Innsbruck: University of Innsbruck, 1971), pp. 262–336.

[17] For the use of this terminology in ecclesiology, see R. Schulte, "Kirche und Kult", in F. Holböck and T. Sartory, eds., *Mysterium Kirche* (Salzburg: Otto Muller, 1962), p. 771. It is used similarly by Hans Urs von Balthasar, *Church and World* (New York: Herder & Herder, 1967), p. 143.

[18] I have discussed this in a monograph entitled, *Holy Church, Sinful Members: A Dispute at Vatican II* (Evansville, Ind.: Sarto House, 1973).

[19] Most helpful insights in regard to the reluctance of contemporary youth (at least American) to accept the reality of sin and guilt, and the

attrition the human being suffers by such refusal are offered by Marcia Cavell, "Visions of a New Religion," *Saturday Review*, Dec. 19, 1970, pp. 12–14, 43 ff. "For guilt, the insight of religion in the West that our capacity for remorse is bound up with our capacity for love seems to me an important one. For guilt, it says, is the only way we have of recognizing, with feeling, we have hurt, or have wished to hurt, someone we love. And love itself was never easy" (p. 44). In this connection Jerome Hamer remarks that the characteristic sin of man today is precisely the "forgetfulness of sin or more exactly the elimination of sin" in *"Il peccato e il mondo moderno," Humanitas*, XX (1965), p. 1162.

[20] That such a relativization of sin is valuable not only religiously or spiritually, but also socially is pointed out by Karl Rahner. This is especially important today, when many are urging not only reasonably acceptable "political theology" (Johannes Metz, for example), but when many are being tempted to a social action reductionism of ecclesiology.

[21] I have developed these applications in "Ecclesiology and Mental Health," *American Ecclesiastical Review*, 167 (February, 1973), pp. 91–101.

The Meaning of Jesus' Sacrifice

BARBARA AGNEW

If the Christian communion is divided and struggling to regain a lost unity, if attendance at one another's Eucharist is a most delicate point at ecumenical meetings, the question of the sacrificial character of the Eucharist is one of the central points of difference. Similarly, reaching a certain agreement on the topic between Roman Catholics and Anglicans and an initial convergence of opinion between Roman Catholics and Lutherans are regarded as hallmarks of progress on the way to unity.[1]

Given the major conflicts that are disrupting nations, and given the critical position of religion itself, opinions about the sacrificial character of the Eucharist may seem hardly worth the time and energy of Christians. Yet for centuries men and churches have been committed to positions regarding Eucharistic sacrifice which cannot be simply swept aside.[2]

Let us admit, then, the power that the question of sacrifice exhibits in Christianity and undertake a new examination of it. It may be putting the question too boldly to ask, "Does the sacrifice of Jesus make a difference?," but is not this what it really comes to? For unless it can be shown that sacrifice really "matters," it would seem better to pass on to more immediately pressing questions. Let us then look at sacrifice from several angles. First, let us in-

quire how it appears to students of the history of religions
and to anthropologists; next, let us examine the degree to
which the idea of Jesus' sacrifice is present in the Scriptures. There we shall find that, as in other areas of Christian thought, much new light can be shed on old questions
by the progress in biblical studies and in related areas. It
can be shown that the character of sacrifice, as illuminated
by anthropology, philosophy, and biblical research, is that
of a fundamental religious act of supreme importance for
Christianity.

ANTHROPOLOGY AND THE HISTORY
OF RELIGIONS

It may come as a surprise to theologians to learn that
among anthropologists and historians of religion there is
no well-defined concept of sacrifice. This underdevelop-
ment is due, in part, to the hostility between religion and
the social sciences in their earliest periods of development
and to the consequent lack of serious interest in religion
by the social sciences. Prejudices against worn-out forms
of Christianity during the late 19th and early 20th centuries were evident; Eliade notes that Freud's *Totem and
Taboo* became "one of the minor gospels of three generations of Western intelligentsia" despite the fact that
totemism had long since been discredited as a universal
and archaic sacrificial practice.[3]

Theodore Van Baaren complains that the terminology
for sacrifice now in use is "unsatisfactory and confusing,"
with neither a precise definition nor a system in which to
organize its many forms.[4] Van der Leeuw says that sacrifice

is among the terms with the widest variety of meanings; Clifford Geertz warns that anthropologists are operating with only common sense notions of what such important activities as worship and sacrifice are, and asks for "a theoretical analysis of symbolic action comparable in sophistication to what we now have for social and psychological action." [5]

The gift, communion, and expiation theories of sacrifice offered by early students of religion still dominate the field. Van der Leeuw sees all aspects of sacrifice comprised under a greatly expanded and nonwestern idea of the meaning of gift. Going beyond the *do ut des* theory of gift, he thinks that it is a means of allowing a stream of power to flow: "We give and receive and it is impossible to say who is the giver and the receiver." [6] Raymond Firth, departing from the gift theory, struggles with notions of limited resources, destruction, transformation, and self-denial in his concept, concluding that sacrifice is fundamentally a symbolic act "of critical significance for human personality." [7] Both Geertz and Firth, then, in speaking of sacrifice, conclude that studies in the function of symbols may provide the only keys to future development in the study of religion and religious ritual or symbolic acts.

RITUAL, SYMBOL AND SYMBOLIC ACT This movement toward the recognition of the importance of symbols and symbolic acts has been set in motion by the growing realization that "what man believes comes more clearly to light in the manner of his acts than his ideas." Yet along with the awareness of the primacy of ritual, there is the "widest possible disagreement as to how the word ritual should be used and how the performance of ritual should be understood." [8] Leach, surveying the meanings given to the ritual of sacrifice, concluded that they cannot all be true at once, and that none of them reaches into the heart of the problem, which is why the killing of an animal should be endowed with religious meaning at all.

Fundamental to any consideration of sacrifice as symbolic act is a consideration of the function of symbolism in general. Since the work of Ernst Cassirer, Susanne Langer, and Carl Jung, studies in symbol and symbolic function have increased in number and influence, and only the briefest statement can be made here of their implications. A symbol represents the signified by making it present and taking its place; instead of a univocal relation between sign and signified, there is a wealth of meaning in the symbol, which reveals ever new aspects of the signified.[9] The symbol always contains a "surplus of meaning beyond what it directly discloses." No interpretation can be exhaustive because the symbol "contains and structures the very reality to which it refers" and also because the transcendent dimension of the symbol enables the mind to surpass the purely empirical.

Thought, in fact, remains subordinate to the symbol: It is interpretation and not translation which is required. The effect of interpretation is not that of making the symbol rationally or logically transparent, but that of deepening and expanding the symbol. A genuine interpretation of the symbol, then, must adopt a symbolic attitude—the so-called "hermeneutic circle." To attempt to repeat in ordinary discourse what symbolic structures express would mean that "we settle for a very limited aspect of the symbolic expression." [10]

If, then, the effort to interpret a symbol in language

alone is doomed to failure, ritual behavior such as sacrifice must be interpreted substantially by behavior, by gestures. The implication for theologians is clear: Definitions of sacrifice, or dogmatic definitions, or statements which contain implicitly definitions of sacrifice are faced with the challenge of the hermeneutic circle. Doctrines which include these definitions are prey to the problem of being unable to express linguistically what is contained in the symbolic act.

In sum, then, there is a shift taking place away from the old theories of gift, communion, and expiation as the meaning of sacrifice, but no single theory has yet replaced them. Scholars in the science of religion and in anthropology admit and regret the lack of work in this area, and point to the use of the structures of the symbolic act as the key to future development, but efforts to analyze sacrifice as symbolic act are very few. Nevertheless, there is sufficient reason for theologians, reflecting on the meaning of sacrifice, to use care in asserting what sacrifice "means" when it appears in a given culture or a theological statement.

SACRIFICE IN BIBLICAL THOUGHT

THE OLD TESTAMENT: SUFFERING IS SACRIFICE In Christian theology, Jesus is said to be himself a perfect sacrifice to the Father. To what extent is this description rooted in Scripture? The Old Testament does not contain a theory of sacrifice; it is an open question. Nor are the sacrifices themselves easy to distinguish apart from the functions they serve, appearing as they do in various strata of the text.[11] Furthermore, it is from the Suffering

Servant, rather than from the cultic sacrifices that the sacrificial implications of Christ's life and death are chiefly
drawn. "It is not too much to say," writes John L. Mac-
kenzie, "that the conception of the atoning and redeeming
death in the New Testament is a development of the idea
of the Servant." [12]

But taken as they stand, the Servant Songs are not at all
linked with the sacrifices of the Temple cult, nor at the
time of Christ did Jewish thought give the songs either a
messianic or a sacrificial interpretation.[13] It is the occurrence of cultic terms such as *āsām* and *nĕpes* in Is. 53:10b
and 12b which are used to explain the identification between Jesus and the Suffering Servant. But without the
long tradition which interprets Jesus' suffering as sacrificial, one could regard such a semantic link as tenuous and
contrived. The Songs are not themselves a description of a
cultic sacrificial act; and in the religious sacrifices of Israel
suffering has no place. We say easily that the Servant's
suffering becomes an offering for sin. But the reverse is
never asserted, namely, that a Temple sacrifice involves
the suffering of the victim or the offerer.

The suffering of the Servant, then, is not sacrificial in its
original content. How then did the Christian community
come to make this theme a predominant element in its ex-
plication of the sacrificial death of Jesus? Paul Ricoeur
suggests that it is due to an almost universally accepted
"myth of punishment";[14] this myth is the commonplace
that if one does wrong, one must pay a price.

Despite the apparent universality of this "myth," it is
not beyond criticism. For there is evidence that the assumption that punishment should be painful and retribu-
tive is at work with seriously objectionable consequences

in penology and theologies of penal satisfaction, where it results in what Ricoeur calls "the sacralization of law" and the "juridicization of the sacred." [15] One must ask what is this myth of punishment that seems so reprehensible in its practical implications and is yet so closely associated with the sacrificial death of Christ?

Ricoeur, following Hegel's *Philosophy of Law*, suggests that the core of the idea exists at the lowest level of law, namely, property rights. If one damages the person of another through damaging his property, the injured person is entitled to physical redress, the return or restoration of the property. But at the level of personal morality, where the offense is directed not at property but at the person or the well-being of another, this law of punishment cannot hold. One cannot seek redress by inflicting like injury. Moral evil is at the level of persons and conscience; physical evil is in the physical order. It is the extension of the law governing property damage into the area of moral, personal wrong which Ricoeur thinks is the genesis of the "myth" of punishment.

Applying this to the link between sacrifice and the suffering of Jesus, we see that it is when the redemptive act of Christ is called sacrifice and is linked to the redemptive suffering of the Servant so that it seems that "sacrifice is suffering" that the myth of punishment begins to make its influence felt. It suggests to preacher and to penitent that the painful agony of Christ somehow rights the wrong of man's sin and that his suffering somehow pleases God. Thus are begotten theologies of satisfaction in which Father and Son are opposed to one another and in which somehow pain is the price of forgiveness. Ricoeur thinks that it is the legalism of both the Christian and rabbinic traditions that have contributed to the perpetuation of the myth in Christian theology and, in so doing, have obscured the more fundamental theme of the covenant on which redemption is grounded.

The Covenant symbol, he finds, offers two metaphors for the interpretation of redemption: the metaphor of conjugal love and that of the wrath of God. These express symbolically the light and the dark side of a relationship which legal systems based on sacrificial atonement (tending to include the myth of punishment) are insufficient to handle. Given this broader frame of reference, the myth of punishment still functions in the appearance of the Cross, but as a broken myth. The Cross is neither fable nor idealized expiation, but the memorial of an event, the event of the disappearance of an epoch of law where it did hold and the appearance of an epoch where the relationship of God and man is in the order of the Covenant. For, Ricoeur points out, punishment is part of the economy he calls "law," an economy which has become part of the past: "But now, without the law, the justice of God is manifest." [16]

Thus when the sacrifice of Christ is interpreted as the sacrificial suffering of the Servant, Christian thought becomes prey to the invasion of the myth of punishment and to theologies of vicarious satisfaction. If, however, the sacrificial death of Christ is viewed under the aspect of covenanted love and grace, the myth of punishment, broken by the death of Christ, yields to the "myth" of divine love overpowering divine anger. The Covenant symbol escapes the materialism and the impersonality of the myth of punishment. While the sacrificial death of

Christ certainly includes suffering, suffering cannot and must not be thought to comprise the meaning of the sacrifice of Christ; the death and its inevitable suffering must be viewed under the aspect of Covenant love.[17]

THE NEW TESTAMENT: SACRIFICE AS META-PHOR In the Old Testament there is no doubt that certain activities could plainly be called "sacrificial," and the Servant Songs, reflected on in Christian time, quickly took on sacrificial implications. But in the text of the New Testament, the use of the term "sacrifice" for the death of Christ is infrequent and allegedly far more metaphorical than literal.[18] The focus of sacrifice in Christian history shifts from a formal cultic activity to the whole work of Christ and his people. Robert Daly suggests that Christian sacrifice is threefold: the sacrifice of Christ, the sacrifice of Christians, and Christians as the new temple. There is a "massive transformation or spiritualization of the idea of sacrifice . . . which formed the specifically Christian concept of sacrifice." [19]

It is the process by which this spiritualization took place which interests us here; our point of departure will be the contrasting interpretations of the terms *thuo* and *thusia*. Behm, in Kittle's *Theological Dictionary of the New Testament*, argues that they are used literally of pagan and Jewish offerings, but figuratively of the death of Christ and of the life and work of Christians.[20] Hauret, a Catholic, calls the passages not metaphor but an element of the continuity and transcendence between the two testaments: continuity as evidenced in the use of Old Testament sacrificial terminology in speaking of the death of Christ and transcendence as manifested by the "absolute originality of Jesus' offering." [21] His assertion of absolute originality indicates that a new meaning has emerged.

But if calling the act of Christ a sacrifice is allegedly so original, one may ask how one can use the language and the elements of Old Testament sacrifice to convey this originality. If the originality lies in surpassing the rites of the old covenant, is it sufficient to use these rites to illustrate this new sacrifice? Or perhaps one should ask under what circumstances one can properly do this? For the profound distinction we perceive between subpersonal and personal beings would seem to demand special care in interpretation of the sacrifice of Christ by the animal and vegetable offerings of the Old Testament.

C. L. Mitton also regards the predication of Jesus' death as sacrifice as metaphorical and he focuses on the end of Jewish sacrifice rather than its specific elements. He suggests that what the metaphor says is that the effects which the Jews sought imperfectly in sacrifice have been realized in Christ:

It is the task of theologians to decide whether these sacrificial metaphors imply that Christ's death is best understood as itself a sacrifice to God or whether they are merely vivid ways of declaring that what the Jews sought to achieve by sacrifice has, in fact, been fully accomplished by Christ.[22]

The superiority of Jesus' death as sacrifice, he suggests, lies not in the excellence of the elements—priest, victim, blood —but in the achievement of the purpose of sacrifice. The metaphor, then, has not made a simple comparison; it has asserted an identity stronger than comparison, allegory, or analogy.

Does metaphor possess this power? The term, unhappily, has not been a felicitous one in theology; it implies a kind of "lesser" reality that lies uneasily alongside the kind of truth that faith claims to assert. To say that an idea is "mere metaphor" has been to remove it from the realm of doctrinal truth.

While a survey concluded that "discipline boundaries have been transcended in a common concern with metaphor among semanticists, anthropologists and philosophers," [23] the question of metaphor has received little attention from theologians. Each of these sciences has been challenged by what is seen to be a special kind of human activity at work in the creation of metaphors. John Middleton Murry says that "a fundamental examination of metaphor would be nothing less than an investigation of thought itself." [24] Baym concludes that "the small purpose of metaphor, that of relating two divergent elements, reflects the larger purpose of reading meaning into life." Metaphor study, he thinks, involves the fuller awareness that "the nature of metaphor is embedded in the nature of language." [25]

The description of metaphor as the relating of two divergent elements, which originated with Aristotle and Quintillian, is limited, according to Philip Wheelwright, by being based upon syntactic and semantic considerations. [26] He prefers another definition:

Metaphor is the synthesis of several units of observation into one commanding image; it is the expression of a complex idea, not by analysis nor by direct statement, but by a sudden perception of an objective relation. [27]

For thinkers like Wheelwright, metaphor is not merely a

verbal device, but a relation which transcends the verbal and represents some universal condition of which the verbal is a significant part.[28] Thus the full description of the function of metaphor in a given writer will rest on his attitude toward the universal condition of reality.

For Wheelwright, reality is two dimensional, a mythico-religious dimension interpenetrating the temporal-mundane: "Man lives always on the verge, always on the borderland of something more." [29] The duality is overcome by a third entity which mediates between the two—language, "in which the knower points to what is known." Thus "subject, object and linguistic medium play irreducible and intercausative roles in the formation of reality." [30]

Wheelwright does not try to define the nature of the transcendental aspect of reality; he simply posits the existence of mystery as the ultimate reality. But since he holds that reality can be known only through language, and since language shapes what is known, he has to identify some unit by which the knowing and shaping is effected, and it is metaphor which he selects, treating it as poetic language. Poetry and metaphor are the result of the tension that arises from man's effort to "express his complex nature and his sense of the complex world." The pressure of finding suitable words to represent some aspect of this tension produces a new language (poetry, metaphor) which "partly creates and partly discloses certain hitherto unknown, unguessed aspects of What Is." The value of metaphor is "its power to reveal some aspect of reality." [31] Language, then, is "representative as well as revelatory of reality"; and metaphor is the unit of this representation and revelation.[32]

Given this understanding of metaphor, what are the implications of saying that the phrase "Christ's death can be called sacrificial" does in fact reveal something about Christ? It would then be possible to agree with Hauret that such expressions do assert something absolutely original about the death of Christ, and yet to agree with Mitton that they are metaphorical. Thus, one could speak of the death of Christ as sacrificial but one would be freed from examining sacrifice literally in terms of suffering, death, victim, and blood. Terms such as priest, altar, and victim, whatever other referents they may have in Christian theology, cannot be expected to render the sacrifice of Christ comprehensible in any satisfactory degree. To return to the notion of symbol, to analyze sacrifice with terms derived from Levitical rites is to try to comprehend in language the "overplus" of meaning which it is the character of symbol to possess; it is to be trapped by the hermeneutic circle.

The New Testament, then, offers but few examples of sacrifice being predicated of Christ's death, and Protestant-Catholic polemics color the interpretations of those few. Protestant thought tends to see the reference as metaphorical; Catholic interpretation emphasizes the uniqueness of the act of Christ described as sacrifice. But it may be possible to bring the interpretations together through a theory of metaphor which presents it as revelatory of meaning rather than a statement of likeness and differences.

Our study, so far, indicates that it may be the failure to respect the symbolic character of sacrifice that allows such elements as the myth of punishment its room to function in explications of the sacrifice of Jesus. Similarly, failure to admit the metaphoric predication of sacrifice of Jesus admits an uncritical use of ideas of Levitical sacrifice to interpret the sacrifice of Jesus, creating a movement from Jesus back to the Old Testament, rather than letting the metaphorical (revelatory) power of the idea produce new meaning.

What light has been shed on the question of this essay? First, having found that the Old Testament offers no theory for its meaning, we have observed that sacrifice is understood as admittedly of critical importance, as full of power, and open to exploration in a philosophy of symbolic act. Finding that the chief source for the interpretation of Jesus' sacrifice as sacrificial is the Suffering Servant, which carries within itself the burden of a "myth of punishment," we have shown that the suffering of Christ may be seen as part of a broken myth rather than a statement of the relationship between God and man. And, in the Catholic-Protestant difference over how New Testament use of the terms for sacrifice is to be understood, we have found a theory of metaphor which suggests that sacrifice may indeed be a metaphorical description but that the very fact of the metaphor asserts a uniqueness in Christ's death.

It would be most useful at this point to make a close examination of how the concept of sacrifice functions in the work of some theologians, to learn if the power and the ambivalence of the concept as presented here is evident. Donald Baillie, for example, would be found to shift the meaning of sacrifice as he uses it with reference to different mysteries—the death of Christ, the redemption of man, the character of the Eucharist.[33] While the shifts may be unconscious, one can trace his efforts to avoid invoking the myth of punishment at times, while invoking it fully at others.

It will be, perhaps, more interesting to consider the work

of Jean-Jacques von Allmen, a theologian of the Swiss Reformed Church. In contrast to the Reformed Church in general, Von Allmen finds himself wholly convinced of the sacrificial intent of the language of the New Testament and the patristic period regarding the death of Christ and the Eucharist.

Von Allmen's premises coincide with the findings this paper offers. He, too, finds the theological term for sacrifice to be ambiguous; noting the New Testament willingness to describe worship as sacrificial, he admits its reluctance to use the term for sacrifice in a directly liturgical sense. While he finds the root of an allegedly unanimous patristic tradition in what he calls "an indissoluble link between the death of Christ and sacrifice on one hand" and the "death of Christ and the Eucharist on the other," [35] his assent to the Fathers' manner of speaking is not without limitation; they used, he said, "sacrificial phraseology."

In any case, this was the sense which the Fathers intended when they used the term sacrifice, knowing full well that it was an unsuitable term, but they used it nevertheless, as though compelled to do so on account of the sacrifice of which the supper is the *anamnesis* and because to renounce sacrificial language in the context would have been to separate the Supper from the passion of Christ and to have robbed it of its meaning. That is why, on the one hand, they emphasized the gulf between the eucharistic sacrifice and the Jewish and pagan sacrifices and, on the other hand, they became more and more accustomed to the use of "sacrificial phraseology" when speaking of the eucharistic life with the help, however, of certain circumlocutions and certain contradictions in the very terms.[36]

The expression "unbloody offering" which he finds first in

Athenagoras in 180 A.D. is such a circumlocution; it describes the Supper, he says, as "a sacrifice which is, and at the same time is not, a sacrifice."

Von Allmen faces the danger of an identification by which the Mass becomes another sacrifice by suggesting that the *epiklesis* is the best means of keeping the *anamnesis* a genuine memorial rather than re-enactment. The *epiklesis*, he thinks, presents God as the one who acts in the Eucharist, rather than letting it seem that the minister or the Church controls the Eucharist. The growth of "sacrificial imperialism" in the Western Church, he feels, is the result of the loss of the *epiklesis*.[37]

There is no question, of course, that the sacrifice of Calvary is unique and fully adequate, so he puts the question bluntly: Why did Jesus set the Eucharist so directly in relationship to this death that it would quite possibly become a threat to its uniqueness? He answers that it was first because he did indeed interpret his death as a sacrifice, but also in order to give his followers an example and a command regarding his work of reconciliation. If he was so little concerned for the uniqueness of his own death it was only because of the fact that it is only by self-sacrifice that one becomes a Christian. Thus, Von Allmen does not insist on the uniqueness of Christ's sacrifice in such an absolute sense that it has no resonance in the actions of men. He does not bow down his head before the awful mystery of Christ's surrender of his life; instead, he regards it as a summons to men to offer themselves to God as living and holy sacrifices. Christ invited his followers "through their own sacrifice to share in his sacrifice"; he "involves and welcomes the Church into his sacrifice."

The moment of the Supper is not a moment in which the

Christian "bears the Cross or suffers for Christ"; the Supper is rather "the channel of the sacrifice of Christians, the sacrament of their sacrifice as it is the sacrament of the sacrifice of Christ." He quotes St. Augustine approvingly: "The Church learns this sacrifice on the occasion of the Supper in which she has seen that in the gift she offers she herself is offered." [38] He is at pains to avoid the dilemma of a choice between a repetition of the sacrifice which threatens its uniqueness and a conception of the Supper robbed of sacrificial power. Agreeing that the former must be opposed, he recognizes the need for an alternative lest worship be "aloof from any oblative movement, isolated from the unanimous ancient tradition and uncertain of the deep and true reasons for celebrating the supper." [39]

Thus, Von Allmen has recovered a sacrificial meaning for Eucharistic worship by accepting a tradition of sacrificiality and then by using dynamic notions of the Eucharist to understand it. He avoids efforts to "dismantle an act"— either that of the death of Christ or the Supper. He concludes that the Word is essential to the understanding of the Supper, but that the Supper is equally essential to the understanding of the Word. The Supper "supplies the authentic key to the interpretation of the Old Testament . . . and for the understanding of word of prophecy in the New Covenant." [40] The Supper "safeguards the ministry of the Word . . . by applying its basic hermeneutical principle."

But if the Supper is the key to understanding the two Testaments, it must be preeminently the key to understanding the central Word of the New Testament—the sacrificial and revelatory death of Christ. Thus the Supper, in which is recalled "the culminating moment in the history of salvation," becomes the means of the appropriately symbolic interpretation of Christ's symbolic act, his death for our sins. By entering into the *anamnesis* of his death and by being drawn into the attitudes it suggests, Christians learn the meaning of Christ's sacrifice by using their own lives to explore it.

Von Allmen, committed to the sacrificial nature of Christ's death and of the Supper in which it is remembered, has recovered for himself the sacrificial structure of the Supper without being trapped in the myth of punishment, or in a rationalism which denatures it. And his method is one which meets the criteria suggested by the investigations of the first part of this essay: Rather than explore the Supper with the "grammar" of Levitical sacrifice or equate it too completely with suffering, he has allowed the idea of sacrifice full play as a symbolic act. He has regarded the power and the reality of the Supper with the intensity and certainty which Hauret intends when he speaks of the absolute originality of the Supper. His conclusion, which must be that of this essay, is that to know if the sacrifice of Jesus makes a difference, one must enter into it through the Supper and, ultimately, by risking the use of the hermeneutic of one's own life, one must discover it for oneself.

NOTES

[1] *Anglican—Roman Catholic Dialogue, II.* (Washington: United States Catholic Conference, 1972). *Lutherans and Catholics in Dialogue, III: The Eucharist as Sacrifice* (Washington: United States Catholic Conference, 1967).

[2] G. Aulén, *Eucharist and Sacrifice* (Philadelphia: Muhlenberg Press,

The Meaning of Jesus' Sacrifice 161

1958). D. M. Baillie and John Marsh, eds., *Intercommunion* (New York: Harper and Brothers, 1952).

[3] M. Eliade, "Cultural Fashions and the History of Religion," in *The History of Religions,* M. Eliade and J. M. Kitagawa, eds., (Chicago: University of Chicago Press, 1959), p. 24.

[4] Th. P. Van Baaren, "Theoretical Speculations on Sacrifice," *Numen,* XI (1964), p. 1.

[5] C. Geertz, "Religion as a Cultural System," *Reader in Comparative Religion,* W. A. Lessa and E. Z. Vogt, eds., 2nd edition (New York: Harper and Row, 1965), p. 216.

[6] G. Van der Leeuw, *Religion in Essence and Manifestation,* 2 vols., trans. J. E. Turner (London: George Allen and Unwin, Ltd.), p. 353.

[7] R. Firth, "Offering and Sacrifice: Problems of Organization," *Journal of the Royal Anthropological Institute* XCIII (1963), p. 12.

[8] E. R. Leach, "Ritual," *International Encyclopedia of the Social Sciences,* XIII, p. 521.

[9] The following development of symbol and symbolic act is indebted to the lectures of Louis Dupré given at The Catholic University of America and appearing in mimeographed form.

[10] Edward Sapir's conclusions are similar: "All symbolism implies meaning which cannot be derived directly from the context of experience." The symbol "expresses a condensation of energy, the actual significance being out of all proportion to the apparent triviality of meaning suggested by its mere form." See *Selected Writings in Language, Culture and Personality,* D. G. Mendelbaum, ed. (Berkeley: University of California Press, 1949), p. 564.

[11] G. Von Rad, *Old Testament Theology,* 2 vols., trans. D. M. G. Stalker (New York: Harper and Row, 1962–65), I, 251; II, 392. J. Swetnam, "Temple Sacrifice: Profile of a Theological Problem," *The Bible Today,* No. 34 (February, 1968), pp. 237–38.

[12] *Dictionary of the Bible* (Milwaukee: Bruce Publishing Company, 1965), p. 793.

[13] G. F. Moore, *Judaism,* 3 vols., (Cambridge: Harvard University Press, 1927) I, 551 and III, 166, n. 255, citing Adolf Neubauer, *The Fifty-Third Chapter of Isaiah According to Jewish Interpreters* (1876), an "almost exhaustive collection of Jewish interpretations of Isa. 53, from the earliest down to the seventeenth century," reprinted in two volumes. (New York: KTAV Publishing House, 1969).

[14] See the papers and discussion in *Le mythe de la peine,* E. Castelli, P. Ricoeur, S. Cotta *et al.,* eds., Actes du colloque organise par Le Centre International d'Etudes Humanistes et par l'Institut d'Etudes Philosophi-

ques de Rome (Paris: Aubier, 1967). The colloquy questioned assumptions such as that made by Gustav Aulén: "The thought of Christ as enduring vicarious punishment is indeed found in Anselm himself, though not in the *Cur Deus homo?*, but, quite apart from this, it is clear that the idea of satisfaction passes over naturally and easily into that of punishment . . ." *Christus Victor*, A. G. Hebert, trans. (New York: Macmillan, 1968), p. 93.

[15] Ricoeur, *op. cit.*, p. 26.

[16] *Ibid.*, pp. 41–42.

[17] In a related matter, the notion that Israelite sacrifice "substituted" a victim in the place of the offerer has been discredited as a theory of the meaning of sacrifice. Whole theologies, especially in the Reformed tradition, have been built upon the notion of Christ substituting himself for us, and these must be reconsidered. See W. Eichrodt, *The Theology of the Old Testament*, 2 vols., trans. A. J. Baker (Philadelphia: Westminster Press, 1961–67), I, 165, n. 2, for a summary of the argument against the substitutionary view.

[18] I Cor. 5:7; Eph. 5:2; Heb. 10:12.

[19] Robert Daly, S.J., unpublished lecture notes, Boston College, p. 3. Daly's work on *Christian Sacrifice* is due from the Consortium Press, Washington, D.C., in 1973.

[28] J. Behm and G. Bertram, "Thuo, thusia, thusiasturion," *Theological Dictionary of the New Testament*, G. Kittel and G. Friedrich, eds., trans., and ed. G. W. Bromiley, 7 vols. (Grand Rapids: Eerdmans, 1964–71), III, 180.

[21] "Sacrifice," *Dictionary of Biblical Theology*, ed., X. Leon Dufour, trans. P. J. Cahill (New York: Herder & Herder, 1973), p. 512.

[22] "Atonement," *Interpreter's Dictionary of the Bible*, ed. G. A. Buttrick, 4 vols. (New York: Abingdon Press, 1962), I, 311.

[23] M. Baym, "The Present State of the Study of Metaphor," *Books Abroad* XXXV (1961), pp. 217–218.

[24] "Metaphor" (1927) *Countries of the Mind: Essays in Literary Criticism* (London: Oxford University Press, 1931), p. 2, cited in Baym, *op. cit.*, p. 218.

[25] Baym, *op. cit.*, p. 218.

[26] *The Burning Fountain: A Study in the Language of Symbolism* (Bloomington: Indiana University Press, 1954), p. 931.

[27] Herbert Read, *English Prose Style* (New York: Pantheon Books, 1953), cited without page number by Wheelwright, *op. cit.*, p. 94.

[28] Sister Eileen Miriam Egan, *Approaches to a Theory of Metaphor* (Unpublished Doctoral Dissertation, Washington, D.C.: Catholic Uni-

versity of America, 1966), p. 133. Sister Egan has examined this synthetic theory of metaphor in terms of the notion of the real in the work of three literary figures, Philip Wheelwright, Kenneth Burke, and Wallace Stevens. Burke sees metaphor as communicating "man's inner motivation, his concealed Freudian depths . . ."; for Stevens, metaphor captures the power of nature (for him the ultimate), which is obscured, through the power of the poet's imagination. *Ibid.*, pp. 119, 121.

[29] *Ibid.*, p. 8.

[30] Philip Wheelwright, *Metaphor and Reality* (Bloomington: Indiana University Press, 1962), p. 26.

[31] *Ibid.*, pp. 46, 51.

[32] R. H. Boyle reaches a similar conclusion from another philosophic viewpoint: He argues that metaphor is an assertion of identity, expressing "in a dark manner that sidelong glance of real being with which our yearning intellects must be satisfied until they are filled with the light of Being Himself." See "The Nature of Metaphor," *Modern Schoolman* XXXI (1954), pp. 257–80.

[33] See the author's work on *The Concept of Sacrifice in the Eucharistic Theology of D. M. Baillie, T. F. Torrance and Jean-Jacque von Allmen.* (Ann Arbor: University Microfilms, 1973).

[34] "Worship and the Holy Spirit," *Studia Liturgica* II (1963), p. 129.

[35] *The Lord's Supper, Ecumenical Studies in Worship* No. 19, trans., W. F. Fleet (Richmond, Va.: John Knox Press, 1969), p. 90.

[36] *Ibid.*, pp. 90–91.

[37] *Ibid.*, p. 30.

[38] *Ibid.*, p. 92.

[39] *Ibid.*, p. 35.

[40] *Ibid.*, p. 27.

PART III

JESUS AND CONTEMPORARY MAN

The Pentecostal Movement
and Speaking in Tongues

JAMES T. CONNELLY

At the beginning of this century the pentecostal movement made its appearance in Kansas and the southwestern
United States. Within a short time it had adherents in
every part of this country as well as in many foreign lands.[1]
Considering its origins and its resources, its staying power,
not to mention its expansion, has been rather remarkable.
Anyone attempting to understand this movement must
sooner or later come to grips with its central tenet: an experience of God for the contemporary believer identical
with the experience of the Apostles on Pentecost as described in the Book of Acts. In pentecostal terminology,
every Christian should experience a baptism in the Spirit
and speak in tongues as evidence of having been so
baptized.[2]

In the past the pentecostal baptism in the Spirit and
especially the speaking in tongues has been dismissed as
the product of excitement and the result of suggestion or
exalted memory. It has also been explained in terms of
social and cultural deprivation. Finally, it has been suggested that there is some psychological maladjustment or
personality characteristic that predisposes an individual to
join a movement such as pentecostalism. Hypotheses put

forward in recent years to explain the phenomenon have become more sophisticated but there is ample evidence that the old presumptions still linger.

The appearance in recent years of a neo-pentecostalism in the mainline Protestant denominations as well as in the Roman Catholic Church in the United States and Canada has occasioned a new inquiry which in turn has led to a revision of earlier judgments on baptism in the Spirit and speaking in tongues. A 1969 statement of the Roman Catholic bishops in the United States[3] and a report submitted by a special committee to the General Assembly of the United Presbyterian Church in 1970 exhibit a wide tolerance for speaking in tongues and profess to see the possibility that it will be a fruitful development in church life.[4] This paper is an attempt to focus on one aspect of the pentecostal's experience of God, speaking in tongues; to review the efforts made thus far to evaluate it psychologically; and to suggest a hermeneutic for dealing with it in the future.

Symptomatically speaking, glossolalia appears to be a dissociative phenomenon which indicates the severance of the associational bonds that normally exist between words and ideas. As such, it can and has been compared with automatic writing, trance states, and visions—all of which can be produced by partial hypnosis.[5] In a nonreligious context it has been diagnosed as resulting from suggestion or from exalted memory, in which case a language or languages not consciously learned are recorded by the subconscious and reproduced under abnormal conditions. Motoric speech which seems to bear many of the characteristics of language has been observed among spiritualist mediums, and the occurrence of a seemingly similar phenomenon in a religious context among primitive people has also been noted although it is not clear that this is the same sort of thing as glossolalia among pentecostals.[6] While it is undoubtedly important and necessary to bear in mind the whole range of situations in which this phenomenon appears, the scope of this paper will be limited to glossolalia in a specifically Christian religious context.

It ought to be observed at the outset that it is difficult, if not impossible, to evaluate a phenomenon such as glossolalia on the basis of written accounts alone without any acquaintance with the glossolalics themselves. Nils Bloch-Hoell, who gathered information about many of the participants in the pentecostal movement at the beginning of this century by interviews either with the people themselves or with others who knew them, is of the opinion that many of the leading figures were neurotics or were people searching for ecstatic experiences and easily given to them.[7] It has been the experience of this writer that the great majority of those whom he knows who speak in tongues are people whose religious zeal in charitable works is and has been admirable, whose practical judgment in matters of religion as well as in business affairs has been and continues to be sound, and who, in his considered judgment, are not unbalanced in their personality.

The means of proper psychological evaluation of glossolalia are twofold. On the one hand, any adequate scientific study of glossolalia ought to be well grounded in empirical data. The serious inquirer would do well to review several experiments in which groups of glossolalics were tested against control groups of non-glossolalics with similar religious, social, and economic backgrounds in order to acquire sufficient information to compose and compare personality profiles for the two groups. Several recent studies of this sort indicate that the three models most often used by social scientists in the past to study pentecostalism are inadequate: (1) movements such as pentecostalism arise where there is social disorganization; (2) such movements flourish among economically or socially deprived classes; (3) there is some psychological maladjustment or personality characteristic that predisposes an individual to join a movement such as pentecostalism. According to the latter model, the movement is seen as a collective solution to individual maladjustments or private problems that many people have in common.[8]

On the other hand, the question must be raised as to whether or not there is a theory of personality integration or function that might allow for glossolalia as a motor-activity that need not be indicative of imbalance. The wording of this question is not meant to imply that until proven otherwise glossolalia is a symptom of imbalance. It takes into account, rather, the fact that since it is not an experience shared by the great majority of Christians, glossolalia is more often than not held suspect and viewed as the result of imbalance, suggestion or illusion. In the following pages several representative attempts to provide such a theory are reviewed.

One of the earliest and most frequently quoted studies of glossolalia in English is that of George B. Cutten, a Baptist minister and educator.[9] While he is not unaware of a fair number of case studies of tongue-speaking in a trance state or under hypnosis, he gives no evidence of having had experience of glossolalia in a Christian religious context and, apparently, had no test data of any sort on which to draw. Cutten presumes that all modern cases of glossolalia follow the Pauline description in I Corinthians 12–14, and that what happened on Pentecost is not clear and, moreover, never happened again. He further assumes that the Old Testament prophets were often in ecstasy and that it is not unlikely that they would use a strange tongue. He admits that prophecy and glossolalia are distinguished from one another in the New Testament but asserts that "psychologically the states were the same and one was apt to run into the other." He is also certain that if there were documents available we would find examples of glossolalia long before the days of Christianity.[10] He concludes that glossolalia is a form of psychological pathology.

Cutten asserts that human nature has not changed over the last two millennia and that, consequently, the correct analysis of cases of glossolalia in the present day will also explain the phenomenon to which Paul was referring. If he is to experience glossolalia, Cutten hypothesizes, a man "must put himself in a psychological state where the controlling apparatus of mind is not functioning, and where the primitive reactions, which usually sleep in the subconscious, find their way to the surface and represent the individual." [11] Cutten makes the distinction between thinking and vocal expression, viewing the former as a comparatively late development of the human mind. When thinking becomes a strain it may cease while vocal utterance may be carried on with ease.

On the basis of this hypothesis, an hypothesis which Cutten never tells us he has verified, he advances three conditions for speaking in tongues, all of them connected with the loss of control by the rational power: low mental ability, excitement wherein the excessive pressure of nervous energy is released via the paths of discharge which are most frequent and least difficult, and illiteracy. Illiteracy is included on the supposition that when appropriate words cannot be found because of a poor power of expression and a limited vocabulary, primitive cries and meaningless syllables will take the place of words. Cutten concludes that when these three elements plus the power of suggestion and expectancy are present "we can prognosticate speaking with tongues as a result." [12]

James N. Lapsley and John N. Simpson have studied glossolalia in a neo-pentecostal setting and have discounted Cutten's hypothesis by the fact that the glossolalics with whom they were dealing were people of intelligence and station. Unlike Cutten, who viewed glossolalia as an isolated phenomenon, they studied speaking in tongues in the context of a prayer group. They observed that glossolalia, when taking place within this setting, served as an emotional outlet for the speaker, an initiation into the group, and a personal assurance of divine approval.[13]

On the basis of their observations and studies by Wood and Vivier,[14] Lapsley and Simpson drew a profile of pentecostals as uncommonly troubled people who are credulous enough to reduce their problems to one global battle between good and evil and to expect its solution in terms of a supernatural intervention. They offered the hypothesis that glossolalia is an automatism in the psychic economy of the individual, a form of dissociation wherein all or nearly all the voluntary muscles are released from conscious control. As such, glossolalia results from a conflict within the personality and serves as a genuine escape from it.

Noting the widespread emphasis on the demonic in both neo- and classical pentecostalism, Lapsley and Simpson suggest that this emphasis is very close to the dynamic center of these movements. They see a link between demonism and conflict reduction and proffer the explanation that glossolalia is an indirect though powerful expression of primitive love toward the parent while demonology is a projection of hate and fear in the childhood relationship. The total experience of being in the prayer group enables the individual to regress sufficiently to express his feelings without ambivalence and this gives the sense of peace and joy to which pentecostal glossolalics so often attest. The demons, moreover, provide an object for the hostility normally bound to the hate and love relationships.

The authors conclude that glossolalia, as a means of dealing with inner tension, is relatively painless and not physically exhausting and they do not regard the glossolalic as mentally ill in the clinical sense. While the effects may be negative or harmful for some individuals, they find that glossolalia seems to help people to stay on the functional side of the thin line between mental balance and imbalance. Lapsley and Simpson conclude by expressing their belief that there is no necessary incompatibility between their interpretation and the Jungian approach but they suggest that the church in its efforts to sanctify the world, would be ill-advised to look to the tongues movement.[15]

Although they describe the procedure of one prayer meeting which they attended, Lapsley and Simpson offer no empirical data of their own but quote selectively from psychological studies of glossolalia and make use of psychoanalytic concepts. They cite no empirical studies as evidence that glossolalics actually suffer from the kind of intrapsychic conflict that Lapsley and Simpson account for by referring to the demonology so prominent in pentecostal theology and worship. Their study, however, strikes two notes characteristic of much of the writing about glossolalia in the 1950's and 1960's, and which quite possibly was stimulated by the appearance of tongue-speaking in the mainline denominations at that time. On the one hand, while they discard explanations of glossolalia which view it as evidence of psychological pathology, they retain suspicions of emotional immaturity, anxiety, or some form of personal inadequacy and undertake a diagnosis in terms of the concepts of psychoanalysis. On the other hand, they take cognizance of the fact that glossolalia is one of several factors in a larger religious movement and treat it in the context of that movement.

An attempt to deal with glossolalia in terms of the concepts of Jungian psychology has been made by Lincoln Vivier and Morton Kelsey, an Episcopalian priest who encountered instances of tongue-speaking in his own congregation. Kelsey limits himself to pointing out that Jung encountered cases of glossolalia early in his career, that he was a close friend of Theodore Flournoy, a Swiss psychologist whose most important work was a study of glossolalia among other related phenomena, and that Jung gives several tantalizing but undeveloped references to glossolalia in his writings. On one occasion Jung remarked that the most likely candidate for tongue-speaking is someone out of touch with the unconscious and on another that glossolalia is an example of the invasion of the unconscious prior to the integration of the personality. Kelsey suggests that Jung's formulation of his theory of the collective unconscious reflects his experience with glossolalics and the influence of Flournoy.[16]

Vivier draws on Jung's thoughts concerning the collective unconscious and his concept of the primary religious experience to lay at least the groundwork for a psycho-religious analysis of glossolalia. He notes that Jung expressed the view that traditional Christianity had so organized its dogma, creed, and ritual that it gave its members only a crystallized reflection of the original religious experience, as was seen in the case of Paul and others. The Christ had become an object and as a result was not completely related to the inner man. Turning to his own test subjects, Vivier remarks that there was a close correlation between the factors of edification, exhortation, and consolation and the role that glossolalia played in their lives. This enabled the subjects to relate glossolalia to the biblical experience of speaking in tongues as a manifestation of the gift of the Holy Spirit.

If this positive evidence is accepted, glossolalia would then be a sign of the impression made by the "original religious" experience as experienced by these subjects. The reason why the dissociation should be present in the form of glossolalia would be found in the association between thought and language. Stating the problem from the hypothesis of Jung's "original religious experience" one could easily imagine that the impact of this experience would quite exceed the normal powers of thought and description with the result that thought and language would become dissociated, and speech would occur independently of normal thought. From the above points, a hypothesis can be formulated which would define the particular dynamic system that acts upon the organism to bring about a dissociated state, as being similar to Jung's hypothetical "original religious experience." [17]

If this can be accepted, Vivier concludes, then there is "evidence of the Holy Spirit being manifested among a group of people, in a particular period of time and history which coincides with the gathering, in strength, of the forces of evil."

Virginia Hine, recognizing that glossolalia is one of several factors in a larger religious movement, has advanced a functional interpretation in terms of the dynamics of the pentecostal movement. Her participation in an anthropological study of pentecostal groups provided her with data that showed glossolalia to be accompanied by conversion, a change in the belief system of religiously-oriented individuals toward a more literal, even fundamentalist, understanding of Scripture and changes in both personal attitudes and social behavior. Drawing on psychological analysis of conversion phenomena by William Sargant, Jerome Frank, Abraham Maslow, and William Wood, Hine puts forward the hypothesis that glossolalia is significantly related to commitment in pentecostalism as a movement.[18]

Sargant pointed out, Hine reminds us, the functional similarities in the processes of religious conversion, thought reform and psychotherapy and suggested that experiences such as glossolalia can produce an effect similar to that of electro-shock therapy—temporary cortical inhibition that breaks up previous mental and emotional patterns and frees the individual to develop new ones. Hine notes that cognitive changes were reported by the glossolalics whom she studied and that most could describe definite physical changes during the infilling of the Holy Spirit and certain other experiences of glossolalia. She does not consider the evidence conclusive, however, that there was a physiological breakdown of the degree which Sargant's hypothesis seems to require, although she allows the possibility of a lesser degree of interruption of normal functioning which would suffice for the effects which Sargant observed.

Frank, expanding on Sargant's theory, suggested that religious experiences serve as a mechanism through which attitudes toward God, the self, and those with whom a person has significant relationships can shift in such a way as to lead to permanent attitude and behavior changes. Both Frank and Sargant posit a physiological state which can be brought about in any individual. Maslow noted the relationship between intense emotional experiences and personality changes, and suggested that such experiences contribute to personality growth and self-actualization. Wood found that his data supported the hypothesis that emotionally intense religious experience is connected in an important way with the process of perceptual reorientation and felt that his Rorschach results indicated that the pentecostals whom he studied were in the process of personality reorganization, changing value and belief systems, and restructuring interpersonal relationships.

Hine's study of social movements pointed up the importance of personal commitment as one of five factors crucial to growth and success.[19] Her study further identified two components of commitment in pentecostalism, black power, and other movements: (1) an experience through which an individual's image of himself is altered and some degree of cognitive reorganization in the direction of the movement's ideology takes place; and (2) the performance of an objectively observable act which sets the individual apart from the larger society to some degree, identifies him with the group in which he experienced it, and commits him to certain changes in attitudinal or behavioral patterns. In church-going America glossolalia can and does function to set its practitioners apart. The author concludes that glossolalia is non-pathological linguistic behavior which functions in the context of the pentecostal movement as one component in the generation of commitment.

William J. Samarin, on the basis of extensive linguistic analysis of glossolalia, has also advanced a functional interpretation of speaking in tongues that treats it as one of several factors in a larger religious movement.[20] Samarin professes to be unimpressed by almost a hundred years of trying to explain glossolalia psychologically. More often than not such attempts have been hindered, he believes, by prejudice and the rational tradition in the West that looks with disfavor on emotionalism in religion. On the basis of his own research and that of others he concludes that pentecostal glossolalia is not the manifestation or correlate of any physical events nor is it a kind of automatic behavior nor a feature of an altered state of consciousness, i.e., an artifact of trance.

Because of the contrary view still held by people with limited information about glossolalia my own view must be stated explicitly . . . that the acquisition of charismatic or pentecostal glossolalia is *sometimes* associated with *some* degree of altered state of consciousness, that this *occasionally* involves motor activity that is involuntary or, *rarely*, a complete loss of consciousness, and that in any case subsequent use of glossolalia (that is, after the initial experience) is *most often independent* of dissociative phenomena.[21]

Samarin goes on to note that theories of socio-economic deprivation, once put forward in explanation of why pentecostal glossolalia occur and now largely disproven, have been replaced by the assumption that there is an emotional deprivation that accounts for tongue-speaking.

Among middle-class westerners, therefore, there is supposed to be a "terrible isolation and loneliness," a definite repression of "religious feelings, aspirations, and ideas" which cannot find adequate expression in "words and wordiness." Glossolalia then is a "sudden chaotic breakthrough" of expression that goes "all the way back to the era of one's most elemental attempts to communicate with other people"; it is like "an infant crying without language," in fact, "a childlike, unguided, and unpatterned kind of speech . . . meaningful to the person . . . in much the same way that the first utterances of a small child are meaningful." [22]

This emotional deprivation is difficult to prove, Samarin notes, and fails to distinguish social from individual psychology. There is, moreover, a patent error, he argues, in saying that glossolalia is like a child's speech. There are some similarities but it is the differences that are crucial. [23]

Samarin's own expertise is in linguistics and his unique contribution is to describe the nature and use of glossolalia. There is no mystery about glossolalia, he insists. Tape-recorded samples are easily obtained and analyzed and they always turn out to be the same thing: "strings of syllables, made up of sounds taken from among all those that the speaker knows, put together more or less haphazardly but which nevertheless emerge as word-like and sentence-like units because of realistic, language-like rhythm and melody." [24]

Glossolalia is indeed like language in some ways because the speaker, albeit unconsciously, wants it to be like language. But in spite of superficial similarities, rhythm, volume, speed, and inflection, glossolalia is fundamentally not language. Its function is not communication: It is not the result of man translating his experiences into sound waves that another person can understand. It is not semantic: The sounds do not denote specific experiences that have counterparts in the physical world. It has no grammar, linguistic system, or rules that dictate how sounds are put together so that all persons in a given speech community can understand and make themselves understood.[25]

Glossolalia is, in short, a pseudo-language according to Samarin. Anybody can produce it if he is uninhibited and discovers what the "trick" is. Glossolalia, therefore, is not aberrant behavior, only anomalous. It is anomalous because it departs from run-of-the-mill speech, not because tongue-speakers are abnormal. Producing tongues is not abnormal. But the belief of pentecostal glossolalics about it, that it comes uniquely from God, is abnormal from the point of view of society and Christianity in general. And just as studies have demonstrated that being sick is not what leads to glossolalia, so also, Samarin maintains, there is no evidence whatsoever to suggest—let alone prove— that glossolalics are all of a single psychological type and that this personality of theirs predisposes or causes them to speak in tongues. It may well be that people of a certain type are attracted to the kind of religion that uses tongues but one does not have to be abnormal or of a certain psychological type to speak in tongues.[26]

Most pentecostal glossolalics, however, will insist that speaking in tongues is the direct consequence of being filled with the Spirit, and that you cannot separate the two events. If they defiantly reject every rational description

and explanation of glossolalia, Samarin remarks, it is because these cannot account for the tremendous changes
that take place in their lives in connection with speaking
in tongues. Let us accept their own testimonials, he continues, as proof of the reality of some change without
quarreling over objective measurement.

Not all of it is measurable, in any case, for some of it is religious
in a subjective sense. One does not measure a "deeper prayer
life" in any scientific way, but devoutly religious people accept
its reality as much as all of us accept the reality of happiness.
. . . A glossolalist accepts this transformation as supernatural,
that is, *caused* by God. If it is a dramatic change—taking place
where one did not expect it or more quickly than one expected
—it takes on all the more appearance of the supernatural. But
none of this proves that glossolalia is supernatural. No number
of "miraculous" transformations will make of glossolalia what it
is not.[27]

To say that glossolalia is not a supernatural language is
not to deny that the charismatist's religious experience is
real, revolutionary, and reconstitutive. Speaking in tongues
may not be a miracle but it does symbolize God's presence
or, if one prefers, it symbolizes belief in the presence of
God. With respect to their religion, Samarin argues, some
people,

are satisfied with allegiance to a system, others are oriented by
its explanation of life, still others enjoy most its ritual and
ceremonies. But there are always at least a few for whom real
religion involves personally encountering the "supernatural" in
some form. It is "felt" . . . and one's subsequent hours, days,
or weeks are affected by this encounter. Reliving this ex-

perience becomes for many people an important goal, and religious practices are valued only if they induce and enhance it. This is what the Pentacostal calls "living in the power of God" or "being filled with the Spirit of God." It means being constantly "in touch with God."

Glossolalia therefore is an important component of personal, affective religion. Whenever a person prays in tongues, he is reminded of how close to him God really is, and he desires (consciously or unconsciously) that God will touch him to make his life different.

From all this we see that the mystery of religion is symbolized, represented, and induced by glossolalia. Like other parts of religion it marks the discontinuity between the sacred and the profane, but at the same time it functions most importantly in the feeling dimension of religion. On these two counts alone we should recognize the legitimacy and value of glossolalia, for it accomplishes two important functions in religion. And it does this without being itself any sort of mystery.[28]

Why do people speak in tongues? Because, Samarin concludes, it is the gesture expected of them if they are to participate in a movement that offers them the fulfillment of aspirations that their previous religious experience created in them.

They too want to believe in God passionately, to know the delight of communion with him, and to see him at work in life. They see evidence of all this in members of the charismatic movement. It is intellectually satisfying, and belief is nurtured by intimate personal relations. This is why they accept the beliefs and practices of the movement. They accept tongues, too, because everything else is so attractive.[29]

As anyone will recognize who has interested himself in

the literature, the preceding pages fall far short of covering all the efforts made to offer an explanation of glossolalia in recent years. The authors whose work I have reviewed were chosen as representatives of various approaches to the problem. In light of their work and that of others whom I have not explicitly referred to, the following conclusions seem warranted.

The work of Hine and Samarin, buttressed by many other empirical studies, suggests that the time has come to call a moratorium on psychological explanations of glossolalia that presume mental illness or imbalance on the part of those who speak in tongues.

The proponents of Jungian psychology claim to be able to offer an explanation of glossolalia that appreciates its value as a means of healing an inner conflict and that allows for the possibility that, as the pentecostals claim, it is related to an experience of God such as was had by men in the early Church. Those competent to formulate such an interpretation should be encouraged to do so.

To understand pentecostal glossolalia it seems to be far more important to study it in the context of the religious movement in which it occurs, to bear in mind its role in that movement, and to compare it as a religious act with others that serve to mark off the sacred from the profane within the affective dimension of religion.

The appearance of the pentecostal movement in twentieth-century Christianity may well give one pause to wonder if religion in de-sacralized societies has become as unconscious as is often assumed. The emergence of a neo-pentecostal movement in mainline churches in the 1960's may very well be an indication of a longing for religious experience. In any event, it should not be so terribly difficult to understand the appeal of a religious movement that offers not a doctrine but an experience of God.

NOTES

[1] Nils Bloch-Hoell, *The Pentecostal Movement* (New York: Humanities Press, 1964); Walter Hollenweger, *The Pentecostals* (Minneapolis: Augsburg, 1972); Vinson Synan, *The Holiness-Pentecostal Movement* (Grand Rapids: Eerdmans, 1971).

[2] John T. Nichol, *Pentecostalism* (New York: Logos, 1966), pp. 8–9.

[3] *Report of the Committee on Doctrine of the National Conference of Catholic Bishops* (Washington: U.S. Catholic Conference Press Department, 1969).

[4] *Report of the Special Committee on the Work of the Holy Spirit* (Philadelphia: 1970).

[5] Lincoln Van Eetweldt Vivier, *Glossolalia*, and unpublished M. D. dissertation (Johannesburg, South Africa: Univ. of Witwatersrand, 1960), pp. 152–66.

[6] George B. Cutten, *Speaking with Tongues* (New Haven, 1927), pp. 176–77; 136–56. See also Morton T. Kelsey, *Tongue Speaking* (Garden City, N.Y.: Doubleday, 1964), pp. 138–46; L. Carlyle May, "A Survey of Glossolalia and Related Phenomena in Non-Christian Religions," *American Anthropologist* 58 (1956), pp. 75–96.

[7] Bloch-Hoell, *op. cit.*, pp. 21, 23–35, 32–33, 66.

[8] The empirical studies upon which these generalizations are based are reviewed in Virginia Hine, "Pentecostal Glossolalia: Toward a Functional Interpretation," *Journal for the Scientific Study of Religion* 8 (1969), pp. 211–226. See also William Samarin, *Tongues of Men and Angels* (New York: Macmillan, 1972).

[9] Cutten, *op. cit.*

[10] *Ibid.*, pp. 1–4.

[11] *Ibid.*, p. 4.

[12] *Ibid.*, 6–7.

[13] James N. Lapsley and John N. Simpson, "Speaking in Tongues: Token of Group Acceptance and Divine Approval," *Pastoral Psychology* 15, 144 (1964), pp. 48–55.

[14] William W. Wood, *Culture and Personality Aspects of the Pentecostal Holiness Religion* (The Hague: Humanities Press, 1965), and Vivier, *op. cit.*

[15] James N. Lapsley and John N. Simpson, "Speaking in Tongues: Infantile Babble or Song of the Self?" *Pastoral Psychology* 15, 146 (1964), p. 24.

[16] Kelsey, *op. cit.*, pp. 196–199.

[17] Vivier, *op. cit.*, pp. 437–38.

[18] Hine, *op. cit.*, pp. 222–25.

[19] Luther, P. Gerlach and Virginia Hine, "Five Factors Crucial to the Growth and Spread of a Modern Religious Movement," *Journal for the Scientific Study of Religion* 7 (1968), pp. 23–40.

[20] Samarin, *op. cit.*

[21] *Ibid.*, pp. 33–34.

[22] *Ibid.*, p. 38.

[23] *Ibid.*, pp. 38–39.

[24] *Ibid.*, p. 227.

[25] *Ibid.*, pp. 73–102, 227.

[26] *Ibid.*, pp. 227–28.

[27] *Ibid.*, p. 234.

[28] *Ibid.*, pp. 232–33.

[29] *Ibid.*, pp. 235–36.

An Apolitical Jesus but Political Christians

JOHN A. GRAY

In his article reporting the 1970 World Congress of Theology at Brussels, Gregory Baum remarked:

We should examine the political implications built into the expression of Christian faith. . . . Today we have become painfully aware that Jesus Christ is invoked by all kinds of people and groups. The priests who are tortured in Brazil invoke him as much as the rightist members of the hierarchy who support the present regime in Brazil as a bulwark against godless communism. What are the political implications built into our image of Jesus Christ? Jesus may be understood as the man of love who asks people to be patient and put up with the injustices of society as the cross they are called upon to bear. Or Jesus may be seen as the man of truth who revealed what was wrong in the institutions to which he belonged and who was sent to prison and even to the cross for this. Jesus may be invoked by people who withdraw from society for the sake of a future life in heaven, or he may be looked up to as the king of the universe who extends his rule over history through the power and influence of the Church. Which Jesus Christ . . . sums up the Christian message? . . . (Which) one is God's saving response to the central problematic of the present age(?)[1]

John Reumann asks the same question:

186

Was Jesus of Nazareth, in his teachings and actions, his life style, and above all, the way he met his death, not merely "revolutionary" but a revolutionist? If so, does Ernesto Che Guerva, the physician who played a leading role in Castro's 'Twenty-sixth of July' revolt in Cuba and who died as a guerrilla leader in Bolivia or Camillo Torres, the Catholic priest who perished as a revolutionary in Columbia . . . legitimately follow in the footsteps of Jesus, and perhaps more properly reflect the real outlook of the so-called Prince of Peace than many of his supposed disciples with their law-and-order outlook in the churches? Or was Jesus a pacifist preaching nonviolence? Or can't we tell?[2]

Albert Cleage, Jr., pastor of the Shrine of the Black Madonna in Detroit, thinks we can tell "the real outlook of the so-called Prince of Peace." For him, the real Jesus of history, as contrasted with the white Christ created by Paul, was the black Messiah of political liberation, with a black God-given mission to win political freedom for the oppressed black nation of Israel from its white political oppressors, the Romans, together with their "Uncle Tom" collaborators.[3]

John McKenzie also thinks we can tell, but his telling is quite different from Cleage's. In a recent review he comments:

We are going to lose the battle, but we will win the war. The battle is the question whether Jesus was and is a revolutionary. The war concerns the basic identity of Jesus . . .

McKenzie, with his usual wry shrewdness, notes:

An increasing number of people cannot be happy revolutionaries unless they convince themselves that Jesus is a revolutionary. If it is true that Spanish revolutionaries in the 1930's turned their machine guns on images of the Sacred Heart, they had a better understanding of the attitude of Jesus toward revolutions than our contemporaries.

. . . I am not sure that Jesus ever promised that nonviolence would "work," whatever that may mean. Possibly he meant that a community of love cannot be produced by the works of hatred. He spoke to the wealthy as well as to the poor . . . Jesus wished to save all men, rich and poor, not to kill them. The image of Jesus with the machine gun does not come off well.[4]

Whether from the left, center, or right, the central appeal continues to be to the classic motivation of imitating Christ, although today that appeal is often formulated in terms of the Jesus of history as contrasted with the Christ of faith. Too often proponents who hold contradictory historical premises and reach contradictory theological conclusions share the same minor premise—that their action is to be based on the imitation of Christ. Thus, on the one hand, there are those who argue against any specific, direct involvement of the Christian churches in directly political matters. Jesus Christ was not a revolutionary. But Christians are called to imitate Christ. Therefore, Christians are not to be political revolutionaries, and the Church (meaning primarily the clergy) is to stay out of politics. On the other hand, there are those who argue that the churches must be engaged in directly political issues, including support of national liberation movements. Jesus was a revolutionary. But Christians are to imitate Christ. Therefore, Christians are to be political revolutionaries; the churches have been inescapably involved in politics (at least to protect their vital interests) and should now be politically involved for the sake of social justice.

Despite all of the advances made in biblical and theological scholarship over the last century concerning questions that relate to the historical humanness of Jesus of Nazareth, many Christians still relate to Jesus of Nazareth almost exclusively in terms of his divinity.[5] If his humanity engages their sensibility at all, it is by way of proving his divinity or re-enforcing an individualistic stance that rigidly separates the religious and the political. When those Christians hear Jesus named a revolutionary, they instinctively feel not only that there is an implicit threat to any social advantages they enjoy, but also that their faith in the divinity of Jesus is being declared false. Furthermore, this double loss is seen to be perpetrated by the very ones upon whom they could rely in the past to be the strongest defenders of both their social advantages and the divinity of Christ, namely, their churchmen.[6] Yet, many of those who do criticize the current social order and who do speak of Jesus of Nazareth in historical terms and for political purposes do not see themselves as guilty of a one-sided reductionism claiming that Jesus is this and only this. Quite the contrary—they see themselves as correcting an already existing one-sided reductionism by calling attention to a central, objective dimension of Jesus of Nazareth that has been obscured in the Christian imagination for some time.

Both sides appeal to Jesus of Nazareth to justify their stance toward the political order and, in turn, their stance toward the political order re-enforces their image of Jesus of Nazareth. At this point, one is tempted to say "I've seen this play somewhere before," or to suggest that we are discussing here what Siddhartha Gautama Buddha would call "a question that does not tend to edification," i.e., one that is unresolvable and does not deal with the fundamentals of religion.

But this play is inescapable for Christians, and this old-new question *can* tend to either edification or non-edification or perhaps both. The reason is that the question of faith and politics is a self-involving question. What is at stake in any such discussion is one's own basic self-identity and deepest convictions. Early in this century, Albert Schweitzer recognized that, like God, Jesus of Nazareth too has been continually re-made in the image and likeness of man, depending on who the man was at the time of re-making. "There is no historical task which so reveals a man's true self as the writing of a life of Jesus." [7]

To answer the original question asked by Jesus himself, "And who do you say that I am?" to answer this question of Jesus' identity is also to answer by implication the question of one's own identity—"and who do you say that you are?" It is to expose, in Daniel Berrigan's phrase, one's own geography of faith. The richer the image of Jesus, i.e., the more multi-dimensional, the richer one's own self-presence. As the painting unveils both the subject painted and the artist, as the gift exposes both the recipient and the giver, so also to speak of Jesus can reveal both him and the speaker. Or with Rudolf Bultmann, there is no presuppositionless exegesis by anyone at any time—including, of course, Jesus himself and his first disciples.

In addition to confronting Jesus of Nazareth as a powerful way of mediating one's own convictions about the mystery of human living, for some of us there is also an intrinsic interest to such questions as: What can an historian say about Jesus of Nazareth as discussed in and through the New Testament Christ of faith? What kind of intelligibility could his historical ministry have had for his own contemporaries in the Palestinian's situation of 28–30 A.D.?[8] Can we validly distinguish (to the extent that it can be historically reconstructed) Jesus' underlying faith convictions from the beliefs by which he brought them to expression?[9] Even granting the inescapability of a multiplicity of interpretations, both in the course of time and at any given historical moment, and granting the inadequacy of any single interpretation as the only "orthodox" one, the question of consistency with the original New Testament witness to Jesus still must be faced.

My intent in this essay is to reconcile two convictions, one historical, the other theological, both rooted in and related to a living Christian faith. The first is the historical conviction that Jesus of Nazareth was apolitical. The second is the theological conviction that a living Christian faith enables and demands that politics be taken with full seriousness by Christians as individuals and by churches.

APOLITICAL, BUT FOUNDATIONAL JESUS OF NAZARETH

A serious reconsideration of (the alleged apolitical attitude of Jesus) is necessary. But it has to be undertaken with a respect for the historical Jesus, not forcing the facts in terms of our current concerns. It we wished to discover in Jesus the least characteristic of a contemporary political militant we would not only misrepresent his life and witness . . . we would also deprive ourselves of what his life and witness have that is deep and universal, therefore, valid and concrete for today's man.[10]

Because of the primary meaning that the term revolutionary has for most people, to call Jesus a revolutionary is to say that he had direct political concerns to reform or overthrow the existing political order. What, then was the attitude of Jesus toward the political situation of his time?[11] Did he understand his own ministry as that of a political revolutionary or political reformer? Was it his ambition and commitment primarily or directly to change the political order and structures of Roman-occupied Palestine in 28–30 A.D.? Obviously, there were political implications and costly consequences for himself and his disciples because of his public words, actions, and lifestyle. He suffered loss of popularity, misunderstanding, and rejection; he was hated by Zealots and Essenes, a puzzlement to the followers of the Baptizer, publicly denounced by Pharisees and Sadducees, and arrested and executed by the Sanhedrin and the Romans. But beyond these political consequences, did he intend social reform or political revolution? Historically, were political concerns his kind of concerns?

It is completely lacking in meaning to ask whether Jesus directly worked for the change of social conditions. We know that for him publicans were just that—publicans—and harlots, just harlots, without his asking who had made them publicans or harlots. He could not ask this question because—to speak in terms of Marxist philosophy—the powers of production had not yet reached the revolutionary stage at which social reconstruction could possibly become a possibility. Thus to ask this question over against the New Testament as an ancient document is unhistorical. . . .[12]

Dorothy Solle gives us the clue: "he could not ask this

question." [13] To speak of Jesus as a revolutionary or an anti-revolutionary in the directly political sense is unhistorical. Historically, it cannot be said that he was either for or against political revolution. While Solle prefers to use Marxist categories to explain the absence of a direct political concern in Jesus of Nazareth, I prefer to explain this absence in terms of his eschatological mentality and in terms of the foundational level of his ministry.[14]

It is not enough simply to describe the many repeated and diverse ways in which Jesus did not conform to the social and religious standards of Palestine in 30 A.D. We also must ask the question "Why?" Historically, in terms of the situation within which he carved out his ministry, he was certainly a man in trouble and at the edge (D. Berrigan), in bad company (Holl), one who lived for others especially the marginal, and who accepted the political consequences of doing so. Certainly, Jesus publicly criticized the powerful groups of his time and the injustices perpetrated by them. But it was not his concern to reform or revolutionize the political order or any order (social, economic, cultural). On the one hand, what he was about was more basic, i.e., foundational. And on the other hand his eschatological perspective precluded such a direct, primary concern for politics. His own "to the roots" faith relativized not only his own political situation, but any political situation at any time, whether of right or left. More basic than any particular institutional or social injustice was the root malaise inflicting the whole situation —the absence of love and faith.

The Palestinian situation within which Jesus lived and carried out his public ministry of preaching the universal nearness of God's gracious and judgmental love seems to have been dominated by one central religious-political question: How was the nation of Israel to survive? It was also dominated by one central conviction: God had to intervene and would intervene soon to restore the religious-political independence of his elected nation as the center of his universe.

The time of Jesus was one of the lowest moments politically and religiously in the history of Palestine. The Palestinians had been fragmented, oppressed, and rendered politically impotent. They were nostalgic for the religious-political independence, which they had last enjoyed a century and a half before during the Maccabean revolution (164 B.C.). As in many national survival situations, this oppressed people was inwardly divided. There were many groups competing for leadership—Pharisees, Sadducees, Herodians, Zealots, Essenes, followers of the Baptizer—each insisting that its way of being Jewish was the only way for the nation to survive. To identify with any of these ways was to take a position simultaneously political and religious. The land was filled with hatred, contempt, polarization—hatred for non-Jews (the Roman oppressors, other goyim, the half-breed Samaritans, the half-Idumean house of Herod), hatred also for other Jews (those seen to be collaborating with the enemy, the illiterate masses held in contempt by the pious and the learned). The other side of the coin of hatred for others, contempt for others, is self-hatred and self-contempt rooted in one's impotence.

Within this survival preoccupied situation, Jesus' faith stance is entirely novel. "The point is not to survive, but to serve. The rest will be given." [15] The point is each is already loved unconditionally, "at the root . . . lies . . .

this gift. . . ." [16] The point is to love all unconditionally. Within a situation filled with hatred for others and self and dominated by groups anxious for the survival of a religious nationalism, Jesus preaches and acts out the alternative way of an active, healing, forgiving, nonviolent love for neighbor with the same love that *Abba* had and with the aim of winning a brother and not defeating an enemy—an alternative way to create new communities.

In this hate-filled, nationalistically charged situation, Jesus emerges preaching the basis for an alternative way of survival and dramatizing it concretely by his own life-style. Against all the dualisms dominant in Palestine at that time—between the nationalistic Zealots and the "non-zealous," between the Essene sons of light and the non-Essene sons of darkness, between the learned and pious Pharisees and the illiterate impious of the land, between the sophisticated, wealthy Sadducees and the poor, between the ascetical, apocalyptic followers of John the Baptist and the unprepared, Jesus discloses the foundational dualism that is to be discovered in the heart of every person, no matter what his position, rank, status, past, sex, religion, race, political allegiances, or moment in history —the dualism between those who choose for the kingdom present already here and now and those who do not. "Turn around and trust wholeheartedly in the good news for the kingdom is at hand."

His way was the way of existentially knowing one was unconditionally loved by Yahweh as *Abba* and thus enabled and called to love unconditionally every other man, woman, and child—a way that was the opposite of self-hatred and hatred for others. It was the way of self-love and love for others uniquely; the way of nonviolence, of concrete deeds of healing service to others, rooted in a trusting, joy-filled abandon before the Father, realistically aware of the cost of fidelity to such a way, and of the price to be paid for putting the worth and dignity of human beings before any institutional requirements, social customs, the expectations of the crowds, or any Messianic revolutionary fervor. The kingdom was already present, not in nationalistic terms, not in military deeds for Yahweh, not in an apocalyptic cosmic judgment, not in wonders and marvels, but in the deeds of love for others rooted in the existential conviction of one's own being loved by God.

Here we have the "foundational why" that makes sense out of Jesus' historical ministry. In addition to this primary foundational concern of Jesus, the absence of a direct political concern on his part is also due to the kind of eschatological mentality Jesus had. His conviction was not only that humans were already loved and that the way of love of every neighbor and enemy would finally triumph, but also that the final, definitive, absolute victory—the Day of the Son of Man—would come soon.[17] Jesus was neither nationalistic, nor a political liberationist, nor directly political, but eschatological, i.e., apolitical, neither for nor against the political order of his time. It simply could not be a direct concern to substitute one political order for another, when the eschaton was imminent. Such as eschatological mentality, which includes a belief not only in the "already nearness" of God's love but also in the "not yet nearness" of the Day of the Son of Man precludes any direct concern for the institutional order over the long haul of history. What counts primarily is the present reality of God's love and the individual's transforming faith, together with the possibilities for new life and the demands for new communities. All else would soon pass away.

BUT POLITICAL CHRISTIANS

Inescapably with the passage of time and the non-occurrence of the Day of the Son of Man, Jesus' foundational faith can be seen to be foundationally or indirectly political and his original eschatological mentality modified. Presumably, the eschatological perspective, although modified, remains intrinsic to the Christian faith stance. For Jesus and the first Christians, its articulation included an expectation about the imminence of the end time. While this expectation is no longer present, the underlying convictions at the heart of this perspective abide, namely, that God will finally at some time act definitely to abolish all forces of evil and to transform human history, and that he will do so from within history as his final gift, disproportionate to but not independent of the efforts of his redemptive co-creators of that absolute future.

Granting this modification, is there anything in the historical ministry of Jesus to which Christians can legitimately appeal as a basis for their serious political involvements precisely as Christians?

It is to be denied that Jesus effected . . . structural changes in the direct sense . . . However, one cannot overlook that, in an indirect sense, the way in which Jesus thought and behaved broke open and changed the social structures of the world in which he lived.[18]

What can be discerned in the historical ministry of Jesus of Nazareth that enables and demands direct political concerns, once the original eschatological mentality is modified? Here we can try to discern, in Gutierrez's phrase, "what is deep and universal and, therefore, valid and concrete for today's man." The answer in brief is not his directly political activity, but his faith stance at the root of all his activities. To imitate Christ is to appropriate his faith stance.

First, the Palestinian leadership's questioning of Jesus' credentials ("By what authority do you do these things?"), reveals one characteristic of the faith stance of this man without socially approved credentials. He had an obvious, direct, and inner freedom of spirit toward all authorities and institutional requirements of any kind, e.g., the centrality of Temple worship, Torah piety and learning, the strict asceticism of the Baptizer's followers, the nationalistic demands of the Zealots and the nationalistic expectations of the people, even the expectations of his own family and the citizens of his home town.[19] This inner freedom is evidenced by his re-defining of his family and of the true children of Abraham, by his freedom of association, by his freedom toward Sabbath regulations, by the non-coercive respect he had for each person's own free capacity to respond decisively for or against the Kingdom, etc. This freedom is rooted in his faith in his Father's love for him and for all men. A faith stance that is characterized by such inner freedom implies that no religious authorities nor social conventions are to be considered absolute. From within his faith conviction about the Kingdom and the liberating lifestyle it enabled and demanded, all human authorities and conventions are of human origin but at the service of the Kingdom, and so subject to change for the sake of the Kingdom. Such a refusal to absolutize any institution is threatening to anyone who identifies himself with an institution as the comprehensive source of ultimate demand and fulfillment for his life. To relativize institutions and authorities is to enable humans to be not only responsive to them but also responsible for them. Thus, while Jesus was not directly political, he does give us a foundational stance relative to and desacralizing of all politics.

If Jesus' first faith conviction is that we are loved, the second is that we are to love "with the same quality and in the same direction as the Father's love for us." [20] The first question for the Christian is always: How can we best love our neighbors and enemies? Obviously, individual Christians and the historic Christian communities have answered or failed to answer this demand intrinsic to their awareness of being loved in various unique ways throughout the centuries. Jesus answered it both by proclaiming the reality of the foundational gift and by concrete deeds of healing and exorcism. With the emergence of the social sciences in the nineteenth century, we are now aware of the dialectic between the institutional order and social circumstance on the one hand and the possibilities for individual realization on the other. Inescapably, love of neighbor and enemy has come to be seen as not only a matter of individuals responding compassionately to each other but also of the political, institutional, and structural order, if it is to be love in deed and in truth.

Correspondingly, sin is seen to be a matter not only of individual actions, but also a dimension of the structural and institutional order.[21] "Social sin" or "the sin of the world" are phrases used to refer to that reality formerly referred to as "original sin." That is to say, human beings are born into a social situation which is not all goodness but a context of incompetence and weakness, of hopelessness and human wickedness, a context of mixed values, which those being born have not created themselves but nonetheless support and preserve to the extent that they interiorize and take for granted such values by the process of socialization. Examples are racism, sexism, and nationalism. The stories in Genesis communicate the truth to us that social situations are of human origin. There are social, economic, political, and national structures that do demean human beings, maintain grave inequities, and reward human selfishness.

Since Jesus' faith stance, as historically articulated, included a belief in the imminent advent of the Day of the Son of Man and excluded our modern awareness of the structural, the direct political concern as an expression of love of neighbor was not possible for him. However, the same foundational faith stance, once informed by the modern understanding of the structural, immediately implies direct political concern as an expression of love of one's neighbor.

In this light, the Christian's deepest political instinct rooted in his faith stance is not to survive, but to serve the advent of the Kingdom announced by Jesus. For this task, the Jesus of history gives no specifics but only his foundational faith stance, which stance engenders those specifics that are both expressive and evocative of the Kingdom, while always remembering that the beginnings of a truly human social change lie in the heart and that any truly human revolution begins with conversion to the Kingdom. At the root lies this gift.

Even if we turn away from the older, individualistic oriented hopes of mankind that pointed to conversion, it is still not correct to think that institutions "created" the man—that is to say, that a change in social structures will produce the new man just by itself. Critical thinking can only deny such a thesis. Nonetheless, under certain social circumstances, a liberated and liberating life style is almost impossible. There are lodgings which systematically destroy the relationship between mother and child. There are organizational patterns of work which . . . exterminate humane capacities, such as the ability to help. . . . If conditions are changed . . . then the conditions for the possibility of another life-style will be present—nothing more and nothing less.[22]

While such a foundation stance demands political involvement by Christians, it can never be reduced to any one political ideology or system. It makes any specific politics simultaneously both important and relative. Depending on the situation, it may affirm aspects of the status quo, reform aspects of the status quo, or revolutionize the status quo. "Political dogmatism is as worthless as religious dogmatism; both represent a step backward toward ideology." [23]

This leads us to a third aspect of Jesus' historical ministry. His stance is not only one of freedom and service, but also one of perennial dissatisfaction since it is informed by a vision of a future communion/community of humans on the Day of the Son of Man, as the ideal at which humanity and God are aiming as they make history together. As Genesis tells us that the human situation is not the way it was meant to be, so the vision of Jesus about the promised absolute future tells us that complete human community is possible and will be achieved. This future-oriented stance

gives no reassurance that "progress" is inevitable, that we will not revert to a new barbarism, that humanity will not destroy itself nuclearly or ecologically. Whatever the significance of the rainbow, the cross is a reminder that the world imaged in *Brave New World* or *1984* or *A Clockwork Orange* is a definite possibility.[24]

Nonetheless, Jesus' vision of this future becomes for us an ideal and basis for the critique and transformation of every status quo. However dependent on and yet disproportionate this ideal future might be to Christian efforts to achieve it here and now,

This community will never be satisfied that it has achieved the Christian order of things because it will always proceed on the conviction that the perfection of the human community can come only as grace, that the Lord himself must bring history to its successful conclusion, because love, which is the stuff of the kingdom, is always a gift, i.e., something to which one responds, but which no one can create as such by his own initiative.[25]

This stance will always be dissatisfied with every status quo and transcend any status quo for the sake of a closer approximation to the promised Kingdom.[26] Jesus stands as one who is free and serves as an agent of the present and future Kingdom for all.

CONCLUDING REFLECTIONS

The twofold appeal to the initiation of Christ mentioned at the beginning of this essay suffers from a narrow unhistorical biblicism. The Gospel, which is the existential foundation of Christian political involvement, is not first and foremost contained exhaustively in a book or any series of books, however canonical. It is first of all, the ever-present reality of God's world-affirming and pure unbounded love. For Christians, Jesus is the original normative witness to that reality, but the literature that records his witness is no substitute for the presence of that reality.

Jesus' stance of faith in the Gospel does not provide us with any specific, detailed, or unambiguous answers to the many complex and delicate political problems of our day. There never have been any specifically Christian political solutions to such problems. Rather, this faith stance rooted in the Gospel enables us to be seriously political on an enduring basis, to face our problems in their full hideousness, and to risk our ever fallible human attempts to approximate the Kingdom for and with all other men, to whom that same Gospel reality is always present, however it might be mediated.

What difference does Jesus make to our political situation? Not by giving us specific solutions to specific problems, not even by giving us the example of a social reformer or political revolutionary, but by witnessing to that foundational reality of God and man, without which being seriously political at all would be impossible. With his stance of faith, with his eschatological mentality modified, and with the critical tools provided by the social sciences, Christians must be directly political and thus part of that birth referred to by the Second Vatican Council, "the birth of a new humanism, one in which man is defined first of all by his responsibility toward his brothers and toward history" (*Church in the Modern World*, n. 55).

Was Jesus of Nazareth political? At the root lies this gift, this uneasy balance and inescapable tension with which the Gospel confronts us. Perhaps we have been engaged in a question that tends both to edification and disedification. And yet we pray, "Come, Holy Ghost, . . . and thou shall renew the face of the earth." The Spirit of Jesus is invoked so that we may renew the face of the earth.

NOTES

[1] G. Baum, "World Congress at Brussels: Liberation," *The Ecumenist* (Sept./Oct., 1970), p. 97. Baum has been concerned with discerning and delineating "the central problematic of the present age" and "the salvational response of the Gospel" to that problematic. He acknowledges that both are matters for discerning interpretation to be realized from within a dialogical process carried on between Christians and non-Christians. In this quotation, Baum could be understood to mean that there is one such image. Preferably, there are many.

[2] J. Reumann in his introduction (p. v), to M. Hengel, *Was Jesus a Revolutionist?* (Philadelphia: Fortress Press, 1971).

[3] Albert B. Cleage, Jr., *The Black Messiah* (New York: Sheed and Ward, 1969).

[4] John L. McKenzie in a book review of George Edwards' "Jesus and the Politics of Violence," *Commonweal* 96 (Sept. 22, 1972) pp. 503–04.

Some other recent examples of descriptions of Jesus of Nazareth as a social or cultural, if not directly political, revolutionary:

(1) "Jesus was hardly a social revolutionary: he does not seem to have opposed Jewish social structures, the Roman dominion or slavery. But he was certainly a cultural revolutionary; he re-defined the prevailing ideas of God, the Kingdom of God and its members, of justice and love. He taught with charismatic authority and dramatized his message in his own life and death, with lasting consequence." Michael C. Mason, "Religious Life—Fossil or Phoenix," *The National Catholic Reporter,* March 30, 1973, pp. 7 and 14.

(2) "As disciples of Jesus, we follow in the footsteps of a Master who . . . laid himself open to risk and uncertainty in opposing certain received patterns in his own culture and in revitalizing and renew-

ing other values; in this painful but exhilarating course of action he learned a critical awareness from the things he suffered . . ." From "American Culture Today" in NFPC's *Priestly Spirituality*.

(3) "Jesus was a social outsider with no respect for authority . . . He did not oppose the power of ruling classes by flourishing swords and trying to seize power, but by announcing the end of all power structures. . . . His way with Torah was to let it hold sway when and where he thought it should and to ignore it when he thought otherwise. . . . Jesus's non-violent attacks against rigidity and authoritarianism made him a true stumbling block to all forms of authority—parental, bureaucratic, educational, economic and military, including the philosophical and theological idealogies that accompany and support them." A. Holl quoted in *The National Catholic Reporter*, March 2, 1973, p. 3.

[5] "We have witnessed a process which Camblin terms the 'iconization' of the life of Jesus. 'This is a Jesus of hieratic, stereotyped gestures, all representing theological themes. To explain an action of Jesus is to find in it several theological meanings. In this way, the life of Jesus is no longer a human life, . . . but a theological life—an icon. . . .' The life of Jesus is thus placed outside history, unrelated to the real forces at play. Jesus and those whom he befriended, or whom he confronted and whose hostility he earned, are deprived of all human content. They are there reciting a script. It is impossible not to experience a sensation of unreality when presented with such a life of Jesus" G. Gutierrez, *A Theology of Liberation* (New York: Orbis Books, 1973), pp. 225–226. A good case can be argued that this iconization process began during the New Testament period and is reflected in the writings of Paul and John.

[6] In the U.S.A., this theological-political position is to be partially explained in the light of: (1) the history of the constitutional doctrine of the separation of church and state, (2) the history of an American "civil religion," and (3) the relegating of religious ethics to the sphere of private morality. But in addition to these factors, there is also the religious sensibility that those who espouse a politically revolutionary Jesus are demeaning the God Incarnate who is to be adored and loved, and not reduced to an improper kind of revolutionary.

[7] Albert Schweitzer, *The Quest of the Historical Jesus* (New York: Macmillan, 1961), p. 4. What is true of us was also true, of course, for Matthew, Mark, Luke, and John; and so inescapably we have the question of the Jesus of history and the Christ of faith.

[8] "What the Gospels give us, inextricably fused together in a single picture is the historic Jesus and the Church's reactions to, and understand-

ing of, him as they developed over half a century. . . . If the early church was led to see in Christ's life more than the first disciples saw, even perhaps more than he saw himself, that is not to say that they were wrong. If they were led to assign him titles to which he himself laid no claim in the days of his flesh, those titles may still point to the truth about him. Even when all the Gospels had appeared, the Church still had further truth to discover about Jesus . . ." D. E. Nineham, *The Pelican Gospel Commentaries: The Gospel of St. Mark* (Baltimore: Penguin, 1964), p. 51.

[9] "It came as a terrible shock to many Christians when theologians at the end of the nineteenth century discovered that Jesus was not a gentle teacher, or exemplary social reformer but a man who really expected the end of the world to come in his time. . . . if Jesus' faith anticipated the imminent coming of a new age which in 1900 years has still not appeared, what possible validity does it have today?" Harvey Cox, *Feast of Fools* (Cambridge, Mass.: Harvard Univ. Press, 1969), pp. 126–27.

[10] G. Gutierrez, *op. cit.*, p. 226.

[11] By political situation, I mean what is meant by the ordinary linguistic usage of this phrase, viz., primarily the order of government with its powers, structures, processes, and parties, as contrasted with but intimately related to the broader economic, social, and cultural orders.

[12] Gutierrez, *op. cit.*, p. 228. Gutierrez goes on to explain that Jesus' rejections of the Zealot's temptation did not mean that he accepted the status quo, for he also repeatedly and publicly confronted the powerful groups of his time and their assumptions. For this prophetic witness, he was seen to be politically-religiously dangerous and executed.

[13] D. Solle, "The Gospel of Liberation," paper originally given at the International Congress of Learned Societies in the Field of Religion, Los Angeles, Sept., 1972. Reprinted in *Commonweal*, 96, Dec. 20, 1972, p. 272.

[14] My position is substantively that of O. Cullmann in *Jesus and the Revolutionaries* (New York: Harper & Row, 1970). Cullmann prefers to speak of Jesus as an "eschatological radical." I agree with Cullmann that historically Jesus was concerned with the conversion of the Individual and not with the reform of social structures. However, I think that more attention needs to be given to Jesus' intent to create the new Israel; cf. C. H. Dodd, chapter v, "The People of God" in *The Founder of Christianity* (London: Macmillan, 1970).

[15] Gutierrez, *op. cit.*, p. 262.

[16] *Ibid.*, p. 206.

[17] Although there is considerable disagreement among biblical scholars

as to exactly when and how Jesus expected the coming of the Son of Man, there seems to be a consensus that Jesus did announce the coming for a near future. Perhaps he did so with divergent or without any further specification of time, and with an explicit refusal to provide more precise details for the simple reason that he did not know them himself.

[18] Solle, *op. cit.,* p. 272. She continues: "Familiar bonds and limits lose their old and natural rank through the new brotherhood (Mk. 3: 31–35). . . . The attachment to behavior such as piety is suspended. . . . Likewise, the socially important division of people by means of education into those who are literate and informed about religious matters on the one side, and those who belong to social classes without this expertise is divested of its dignity and significance. . . . Jesus associated with women —that is to say, with declassified persons in regard to social status and religion." When she says, "the way in which Jesus thought and behaved broke open and changed . . . ," one should add the adverb "eventually." As H. Chadwick points out: "The paradox of the (early Church) was that it was a religious revolutionary movement, yet without a conscious political ideology; it aimed at the capture of society throughout all its strata but was at the same time characteristic for its indifference to the possession of power in this world. . . . this non-political, quietist, and pacifist community had it in its power to transform the social and political order of the empire. There is no reason to think that the early Christian movement was ever a political revolution manque, or that the history of the Church can be told in terms of bourgeois leaders taking over a proletarian uprising and diverting it into innocuous other-worldly mysticism. Such theories can be maintained only by violent and selective use of evidence. But it is certainly true that this essentially religious movement had deep social and political potentialities, many of which were not fully realized in the Roman imperial period." *The Early Church* (Baltimore: Penguin, 1967), pp. 69 and 72.

[19] See G. Bornkamm, chapter III, "Jesus of Nazareth," in his *Jesus of Nazareth* (New York: Harper and Row, 1959), for an excellent, critically aware treatment of the distinctive "otherness" and intrinsic authority possessed by Jesus from within his historical situation.

[20] See C. H. Dodd, *The Gospel and Law* (New York: Columbia Univ. Press, 1970).

[21] See G. Baum, *Man Becoming* (New York: Herder & Herder, 1970).

[22] Solle, *op. cit.,* p. 272.

[23] Gutierrez, *op. cit.,* p. 237.

[24] J. Gray, "Christian Image of Man Fully Alive," in *The Living Light,* May, 1973.

[25] R. McBrien, *Do We Need The Church* (New York: Harper & Row, 1969), p. 206.

[26] "The Kingdom of God is always both an ideal and an embodied actuality. The Christian is always called upon to witness to the truth, to renew the face of the earth, yet he always knows that the Kingdom is yet to come. As a result, 'the Christian is both called to build the Kingdom of God and to build it now, but at the same time to be critical of any existing social order as not yet the final and perfect community.' So the Christian is in the world and not of it; he is never fully at home in any age or country, yet he must take his age and country seriously. So Christianity is a social position and a revolutionary one, for it demands a negative critique and action . . . and at the same time positive projecting and building anew (concrete political action to find and develop alternatives) . . . the Christian must be actively involved in building a world more true to man's dignity and humanity, but he can never give his particular version of the new order the full weight of his religious faith." David J. O'Brien, *The Renewal of American Catholicism* (New York: Oxford Univ. Press, 1972), pp. 226–227.

Death and the Meaning of Jesus

JOSEPH A. LA BARGE

It is almost impossible today not to notice that a great many people are talking, writing and thinking about death.[1] Bolstered by increasingly frequent coverage in the press, on television, and in our educational curricula, we seem to be witnessing what amounts to a kind of "consciousness raising" on the topic of man's mortality.

The observation comes easily that death has been with us from the beginning, and that it has been understood in diverse ways by numerous cultures. Yet to explain our present concern with death as just one more in a long list of efforts to cope with a permanent part of life is, I believe, to miss much of what is being said these days. For the premise that seems to be implied in much of the present discussion is that death is different because life is different; the basic conditions of life have changed so markedly from pre-modern times that it naturally has affected our appreciation of death. A cursory perusal of some of the conditions affecting the quality and quantity of life both yesterday and today might shed some light on this.[2]

Perhaps the most easily recognizable life-controlling factor of the past was the generally limited life expectancy among most peoples. Mortality rates were high for infants, mothers giving birth, and anyone susceptible to serious disease. Such a precarious hold on life brought people into frequent first-hand contact with death—its sights, its smells, and its sounds. Over the years men frequently expressed their awareness of death as an imminent possibility in a variety of ways, but the late medieval period stands out as a time when interest in death reached the point of near obsession. Theodore Spencer writes of these times:

More than any other period in history, the late Middle Ages were preoccupied with the thought of death. In Northern Europe for two hundred years—from the middle of the fourteenth century to the middle of the sixteenth—death was the favorite topic of preachers and moralistic writers, it was one of the most common subjects for popular art, and if a man of the period followed the prevailing doctrine, there was no object so frequently or so vividly before his mind's eye as the skeleton he would one day become.[3]

During this period "an everlasting call of *memento mori* resounds through life." [4] This was also the time when the Black Death ravaged most of Europe, destroying more than 20,000,000 people,[5] and inspired artists to produce some of the most macabre images of death:[6] the Dance of Death, the Triumph of Death, the Art of Dying (*Ars Moriendi*) and the *Quattuor hominum novissima*—the four final experiences awaiting man, of which death was the first.[7]

Death was seen as that which exposed the vanity of life for all to see. As the great equalizer among men of all classes, its message was that neither power nor virtue gave certain protection against an early and possibly painful demise. Carla Gottlieb comments on the implications of this for an understanding of death.

That the conduct of the individual in his earthly life has no influence upon his fate is a disturbing and dangerous thought. The example of Christ, the martyrs, and Job do little to assuage the damage it causes to our morale. Doubts about the existence of God are created; these in turn lead to fear of the beyond.[8]

And if fear of death was so strong, fear of a sudden death was even stronger. "To die suddenly was to be deprived of all the rites of the Church. Without the religious *viaticum*, those black devils which hovered about every deathbed would have it all their own way, and the miserable soul would be hurried off to hell." [9]

Situating our modern contact with death against this backdrop of man's older relationship to death, it is easy to see a dramatic contrast. Compared to medieval times, life expectancy in much of the world today (particularly Western countries) is noticeably greater than in the past.[10] From this observation it is easy to conclude that it is "unnatural" to die young. The claim is frequently made that ours is a youth-oriented society. So many of the products advertised in our media try to seduce us with promises to make us look and feel young—away with gray hairs, crowsfeet, sagging paunch and jowls. It is easy to conclude that if death and youth are mismatched partners, then so too for us who imagine ourselves preserved by the elixirs of a turned-on generation. And as a small but growing number of people are reminding us, when so many gather to worship at the shrine of youth, those who can no longer pretend know that they are *old*, and share among themselves "a kind of shameful secret that it is unseemly to mention." [11]

Our ancestors were frequently exposed to their children,

friends, and elders dying around them, but we are rather safely removed from that kind of contact with death. As with so many other things in our culture, dying and death have been entrusted to a select group of highly trained specialist professionals: physicians, nurses, clergymen, and morticians. Our participation is mostly marginal, and if we really find it distasteful we need not participate at all.

Perhaps most noticeable of all man's modern achievements is the tremendous growth in scientific and technological know-how. So many dreams have become reality that we find ourselves wondering whether there really are any limits to what man can do. Such advances have not simply changed our world; they have altered our expectations of what can be done. The impression seems to be widely shared that given enough money and trained manpower, even death can be conquered; technological answers can be found for all life's problems. This might help to explain in part why resistance to death seems to be so strong in the West, particularly the United States, where technology is valued so highly. In fact Arnold Toynbee has even gone so far as to suggest that in some people's minds, "death is Un-American. For if the fact of death were once admitted to be a reality even in the United States, then it would also have to be admitted that the United States is not the earthly paradise that it is deemed to be (and this is one of the crucial articles of faith in 'the American way of life')." [12] One could further wonder whether this country's supposed image of itself as invincible in war makes it more difficult to come to terms with death.

Finally, we seem to be set apart from ages past by our participation in a pluralistic society no longer held together by a common set of myths and symbols.[13] And with our religious symbol systems in such disarray, the meaning of death becomes much more problematic.[14]

These factors seem to set us apart from our progenitors and prompt us to see death as not the threatening problem it used to be, yet there are many other reasons which draw us nearer to death today. A number of death-related developments come quickly to mind which might account for the present fascination with (as they say in the trade) "passing on." There are the advances in medicine which have raised a host of pressing and perplexing questions regarding the "moment" of death, "dying with dignity," the nature of life sustained nearly totally by mechanical means, etc. In addition, more than ever before we face the prospect of total annihilation through nuclear and biological weapons which have made "overkill" almost a household word.

We have shielded ourselves rather effectively from "natural death" only to find ourselves confronted more and more with "unnatural" violent death: murder, muggings, and rape. There is finally the growing realization that our very way of life contains lethal elements: the polluted air we breathe and the water we drink, the slaughter on our highways, the chemicals we pour into our bodies. Our contacts with death are different in many respects from those of medieval man, but make no mistake about it, death is still very much on our minds.

Death is a very live topic, yet the approach we take to it frequently seems to be ambivalent. Some say that to dwell on death is sick or morbid; yet others insist that there is something equally unhealthy about refusing to consider it at all. Death can be seen simply as a biological fact, much like the period at the end of a sentence, or it can be that

one absolute in life which shapes everything else. It has
been suggested that death destroys all our achievements
and annihilates all our values, but it has also been maintained that death transfigures those same values and raises
them to a new level of importance and meaning. Some
have claimed that ours is a death-denying culture, and in
many ways this seems to hold true. As an undeniably important part of life it is difficult not to speak about death,
yet we do seem to try—at least we try to avoid calling it
by its proper name. And in so doing we have concocted
an impressive and by now familiar list of euphemisms to
assist us.[15]

Denying death in the midst of life can be an event of no
little consequence. Only a few years ago British anthropologist Geoffrey Gorer advanced the fascinating thesis
that there is an enlightening analogue between our present
denials of death and our misgivings over sex.

At present death and mourning are treated with much the same
prudery as sexual impulses were a century ago. Then it was
held, quite sincerely, that good women, or ladies, had no sexual
impulses, and that good men, or gentlemen, could keep theirs
under complete control by strength of will or character so that
it need be given no public expression, and indulged, if at all, in
private as furtively as if it were an analogue of masturbation.[16]

Thus, "one mourns in private as one undresses or relieves
oneself in private, so as not to offend others." [17] The implications of Gorer's observations are as intriguing as they are
alarming. For while there is still no widespread agreement
on how to handle sexual urges, there *is* a growing recognition that human beings do have them. But, laments Gorer,
"there is no analogous secular recognition of the fact that

human beings mourn in response to grief, and that if mourning is denied an outlet, the result will be suffering, either psychological or physical or both." [19] And as pornography seems to flourish in periods of the greatest prudery, it would seem that death is now replacing sex as the topic frequently considered as obscene—too horrible to contemplate or discuss. Suppressed in this way, death spawns its own kind of pornographic expression. It titillates our curiosity, fires our private fantasies, and "those whose power of fantasy is weak, or whose demand is insatiable, constitute a market for the printed fantasies of the pornographer" [19]—be he dealing in sex or death or both.

The point to be taken from these varied reflections is that a person who effectively denies death also runs the risk of denying life. For in the midst of life we are in death. The cult of life involves the cult of death.

This situation is of special concern for religion, which addresses itself to the meaning of life and also, perforce, to the meaning of death. As Peter Berger reminds us, "every human society is, in the last resort, men banded together in the face of death. The power of religion depends, in the last resort, upon the credibility of the banners it puts in the hands of men as they stand before death, or more accurately, as they walk, inevitably, toward it." [20] And for Christians, death takes on added importance. For without wishing to prejudice the importance of the Resurrection, Ladislaus Boros reminds us that "it is a constant conviction of the Christian Church, founded on the statements of Scripture, the tradition of the Fathers and the general teaching of the Church, that Christ saved us by his death, not in any other way." [21]

A number of points seem to be stressed in the scriptural

understanding of death, particularly the New Testament, where death is presented as that which is the consequence of Adam's sin, part of the universal fate of mankind, and that which brings to completion man's status as *homo viator*. From a theological standpoint this is not to insist, of course, that had there been no original or personal sin man would have continued to live forever. Rather, as Karl Rahner suggests, "he would surely have experienced an end to his life, but in another manner; maintaining the integrity of his bodily constitution, he would have conducted his life immanently to its perfect and full maturity . . . through a 'death' which would have been a pure, active self-affirmation." [22]

But death as it exists for most men is not this pure, active self-affirmation of life. It is an event which is approached with fear and trepidation. Donal Dorr offers a possible theological explanation for this fact in light of the biblical emphasis on death and sin.

If there were no sin in the world, no danger of sin in our lives, then the ambiguity of our actions would no longer exist, or at least would no longer be frightening. What terrifies us is the possibility that even what appears to be our best-intentioned actions may spring from a corrupted character and sinful motives. That such self-deception is possible we know from our own experience and the evidence of its effects in others. We fear that death may intervene while we are living in smug, self-inflicted blindness. This is the primary source of the terror of death. . . . But far more serious is the rational dread of death. Its *point of insertion* is the ambiguous nature of our choices and actions, the fact that we cannot eliminate doubt about the purity of our intentions and the uprightness of our characters. But the real cause of the dread is sin as a pos-

sibility and a reality in our lives. If sin is the cause of the dread
of death, we can truly say that sin is the cause of death itself.
For death seen precisely as a human reality is not merely the
end of life on earth but the terrifying thing that is feared all
through life because it may reveal our lives to have been a sham
and may seal the creation of a monument of folly and evil.[23]

It is important to understand this moral dimension which
makes death so tragic. If it is forgotten, salvation becomes
a purely physical event: Man is saved from death rather
than sin, and is more concerned with personal immortality
than with reconciliation with God.

It is clear that Paul understood sin as intrinsic to death
and not as something arbitrarily and artifically tacked on.
For Paul, man's "sinful passions evoked by the law worked
in our bodies, to bear fruit for death" (Rom. 7:6). "For
sin pays a wage, and the wage is death" (Rom. 6:23).
Commenting on Paul's understanding of sin and death,
John Macquarrie writes: "On this view, death is nothing
but the working out of sin itself, and by 'death' is understood not merely physical extinction but a gradual process
of disintegration reaching to the entire person, a process
which may be described as 'loss of being.' " [24]

Yet for Paul death is not something purely and simply
negative. He also speaks of being "crucified with Christ"
(Gal. 2:20), being "baptized into his death" (Rom. 6:3),
confident that 'if we have become incorporate with him in
a death like his, we shall also be one with him in a resurrection like his" (Rom. 6:5). Dying of this sort is not a
process of disintegration leading to a loss of being. Rather
death is affirmed positively, not as the loss of being but the
fulfillment of being.[25] Death is not something that will
simply "happen"; death is rather something one delib-

erately and personally accepts as having the potential for becoming a positive factor in one's existence.

When Paul (and other Christian writers) spoke of death as fulfillment and not simply as loss of being, it is quite clear that they had before their minds the death of Christ. Pursuing this point, Macquarrie remarks that "by a remarkable transformation, Christ's passion and death had become for the Church the manifestation of spiritual life and power, and this had made possible an altogether new understanding of the significance of death in Christian existence, a new grasp of the paradox that through losing life men may find it." [26] Thus for the Christian community, the death of Jesus became the paradigm for finding positive meaning and life in death.

That death which Jesus suffered prior to his being raised by the Father is valued by Christians as the supreme act of reconciling man with God; it was not something which Jesus merely endured, but that which he freely undertook in obedience to the will of the Father (Phil. 2:8; Mk. 14:36; Mt. 26:39; Lk. 22:41). But even this death was not immune from moments of darkness. The agony in the garden, the abandonment by his disciples, the cry of dereliction, his parting words to his mother—all these serve to remind us of what the early Church proclaimed: He was "really born, ate and drank; was really persecuted under Pontius Pilate; was really crucified and died, in the sight of heaven and earth and the underworld." [27] Here there lurks that element of negativity apart from which we could not talk of Jesus enduring the cross or suffering under Pilate. How are we to reconcile those positive and negative aspects which are part of the death of Jesus and the Church's belief?

The resolution of such a question can most appropriately begin with the affirmation of John's prologue: The Word became flesh. Or, phrased somewhat differently, the Word took on the conditions of a limited and finite life. It is significant that theologians have generally followed the lead of Scripture and have focused on the relation between death and sin. However, for the purposes of our present discussion we would prefer to explore finitude as an existential structure of human existence, which will lead us into further thoughts on the subject of the death of Jesus. For this consideration of the relationship between existence as finite and death, we turn to the thought of the great German philosopher, Martin Heidegger.[28]

The central theme in Heidegger's thought is always man and being as experienced by man in his daily existence. Especially in *Being and Time*, death is important because it is that which reveals the ephemeral, limited, and finite quality of human existence.[29] Man exists as this being-mortal, as being-unto-death. Death forms the ultimate possibility of man's being. Yet death is a possibility of existence in a unique way, since it subsumes and encompasses all other possibilities in itself. As James Demske quips, "put crudely, the last thing that . . . [man] can be is dead."[30] Or as Heidegger himself puts it, "the issue is nothing less than Dasein's Being-in-the-world. Its death is the possibility of no-longer-being-able-to-be-there."[31] "Death is the possibility of the complete impossibility of Dasein,"[32] "the possibility of the impossibility of any existence at all."[33]

Man perceives death as the end of his being-in-the-world, which as such, is considered the greatest possible evil because it implies the loss of all that is familiar and secure. As Demske sees it, death is that which "overpowers all . . . [man's] power, renders every perfection imperfect, and ultimately exiles man from everything with which he is familiar and at home." [34]

Man runs from death only to find that "he who flees in the face of death is pursued by it even as he evades it." [35] As Heidegger observes, quoting an old German proverb, "as soon as man comes to life, he is at once old enough to die." [36] Realizing that death cannot be outstripped, an effort is made to forget about it, to cover it up, to pretend it is not there. Heidegger calls such an attitude inauthentic because it tries to deny that about which there can be no denying. Or as Demske suggests, "the desire to put off death into an indefinite future is inauthentic precisely because the possibility of death cannot be put off; death is possible at each and every instant." [37] Authentic existence for Heidegger is accepting life as evanescent, finite, and culminating in death. Seen in this light, death is not simply that which happens to man; it is that which he embraces as "the uttermost of man's potentialities, embracing and uniting all the other potentialities he has." [38] To live is to be on the way toward death as that end which gives life its unity. As Demske points out,

Death is not an event which puts an end to life, but an existential-ontological determination of existence: as such, it is a part of life itself. It is not something occurring just at the end of a man's life, but something always present, from the very beginning of life, as a constitutive element of existence. Thus death lies not in the future, but in the here and now, affecting every act in which existence is realized. It is thus seen not by looking ahead, but by re-flecting, i.e., looking *back* upon existence. Accordingly, the question of what will come *after* death does not arise.[39]

Heidegger's thinking will strike many as strange or even bizarre, especially if serious attention is not given to the phenomenological basis and method which he employs. Important for our purposes here is to point out that he sees death in a positive light because it provides the possibility of an absolute in a life otherwise characterized by relativity.

Returning to the death of Jesus, we have identified our task at hand as providing a more adequate explanation of how he freely embraced his death yet did so not without a struggle.

Paul states in Romans 8:3 that God sent his own Son into the world "in the likeness of sinful flesh and for sin." Theologians have traditionally suggested that although Christ himself was sinless in becoming man, he assumed a sinful human nature, sinful flesh. While this manner of speaking is certainly correct, it can lead into a docetic kind of extrinsicism. As Macquarrie complains, "the expression 'sinful flesh' inevitably suggests that sin is a property inhering in some abstraction called the 'flesh'; whereas sin is in truth a possibility in which a concrete existent stands." [40] "But," as Macquarrie continues, "if what is meant by saying that Christ assumed sinful flesh is that he stood in the possibility of sin and was involved in the relativities of the human situation, this must be conceded in spite of the traditional Christological doctrine of his impeccability (i.e., that because of the *aseity* of the divine nature, Christ had not even the possibility of sinning)." [41]

This leads us to suggest that Jesus' life with us "in the flesh" is a way of affirming his sharing with us the relative and finite character of human existence.[42] This does not necessarily prejudice the discussion of Jesus' sinlessness since finitude, not sin, is basic to man's being. Hence, "the dark side of Jesus' death arises out of his genuine participation in finite existence, so that while his death was supremely creative, it was also experienced as the creaturely loss of being-in-the-world. And while it was the sublime *act* of saving love, it was also the *passion* that had to be met (again *pace* the traditional Christology) in the finite 'theological virtues' of faith and hope."[43]

The darkness we experience in death is no doubt due in large measure to the connection of death with sin. Yet there also seems to be a kind of darkness inherent in human existence itself insofar as it is finite and limited. For death gives life the stamp of finality. As Donal Dorr explains it,

Death is the end of human life as we know it, because life in this world is essentially the process of making up one's mind about what one wishes to be. Death seals irrevocably each man's particular decision about what one wants to be. Life after death is a matter of living the life one has chosen—living it in an eternity that is not an indefinite extension of time, but the unified "now" of a spirit who has completed his own creation.[44]

And as Macquarrie adds, "to die is not to relinquish this or that possibility, but to relinquish all possibilities other than dying itself; and for this would be required the highest act of faith matched by a corresponding abyss of doubt."[45]

The Council of Chalcedon proclaimed the consubstantiality of Christ both with the Father and with mankind.

Most often we think of this in terms of our humanity and our lives; there seems to be no reason to exclude death.

Death was for Jesus and is for us the only possibility amid the relativities of a finite existence to establish in a permanent and absolute way the direction and quality of one's life. Seen as life's final task to be personally accomplished, death extends throughout the whole of life. Applying this to Jesus, Rahner suggests that this

makes it easier to comprehend how the life and death of Christ in their redemptive significance also form a unity. His life redeems, inasmuch as his death is axiologically present in his entire life. And in so far as any moral act of man is to be considered as a disposing of his entire person with regard to his interior destiny, and in so far as such a disposition receives its final character only in death, it is clear (on the suposition that Christ assumed the flesh of sin and death) that we cannot really say that Christ could have redeemed us through any other moral act than his death, even had God been disposed to accept some other act. Therefore, it is just as correct to say that his obedience is redemption, because it is death, as it is to say that his death effects our redemption, because it is obedience.[46]

Or, in the words of Michael Schmaus,

by willingly going to his death he recapitulated that willingness to obey the Father which he had exercised throughout his entire life. In this he realized his own perfection, for in this most complete act of obedience he transcended himself in the direction of God without reservation and thus attained himself in a perfected way. A sign of this was the resurrection.[47]

Our purpose here has not been to separate Jesus' death from his resurrection, turning the calendar back to a time when the crucifixion was seen as central and the Resurrection was a kind of apologetical underpinning. Rather we have tried to link the death of Jesus with his life, that life leading to death and culminating in the Resurrection. In so far as death is the culmination of life, we can say that the death (and resurrection) of Jesus is the bringing to mature fruition of the Word become flesh. The Incarnation, in other words, is a gradual process perfected in death.

The Christian who as a being-toward-death sees his life as lived in Christ must also see himself as a being-toward-the-death-of-Christ. As Rahner points out, "those who die in faith are not 'dead in Christ' only because they lived in Christ, but also because their dying itself was in Christ." [48]

In a very special way man's relationship to the life and death of Jesus achieves physical and social visibility in the sacramental actions of the Church. Of special significance are Baptism, the Eucharist, and the Anointing of the Sick as they relate to the beginning, growth, and decline of man as a being-towards-death. A theology that attempts to explicate these symbols and their rituals and relate them to death must, of course, express itself in ways understandable to modern man, and study seriously the images which dominate man's consciousness today. And when it comes to the power of the imagination to deal with death, we as Westerners and as Americans find ourselves at a disadvantage.

For, as William Lynch remarks, "there is nothing we are imagining or can imagine less successfully than death. Therefore we cannot cope with it." [49] Lynch continues his observations on our American malaise:

The image of death as passivity and helplessness may well be the great American fear. The American has not yet been helped by our artists to handle images of passivity. He has only demeaning and corrupt images of the passive, of not being able, like Horatio Alger, to do all things. And such are his images of waiting, or doing nothing, or being dependent. The American is not equipped, therefore, with an imagination with a set of images, which would tell him that it is all right to lie down in good time and die, dependently leaving it to God to raise him up again.[50]

Yet even locating and explicating more adequate symbols and images to assist us in coming to terms with deaths will not resolve completely the paradox of life and death. We will then only be re-stating (and re-living) more faithfully the message Jesus gave us as he made his way to Jerusalem and his own death: "If any man would come after me, let him deny himself and take up his cross daily and follow me. For whoever would save his life will lose it; and whoever loses his life for my sake, he will save it" (Lk. 9:23–24).

NOTES

[1] For an indication of the proliferation of death-related literature, especially in recent times, see: Robert Fulton, ed., *Death, Grief and Bereavement: A Chronological Bibliography, 1843–1970* (Minneapolis: University of Minnesota Center for Death Education and Research); Joel J. Vernick, ed., *Selected Bibliography on Death and Dying* (Washington: U.S. Department of Health, Education and Welfare). A number of journals also focus on this area. See: *Journal of Thanatology* (Health Sciences Publishing Corp., 451 Greenwich St., New York, New York, 10013), and *Omega* (Greenwood Periodicals Co., 51 Riverside Ave., Westport, Conn., 06880).

[2] Cf. Robert Kastenbaum and Ruth Aisenberg, *The Psychology of Death* (New York: Springer Publishing Co., 1972), pp. 191–203.

[3] Theodore Spencer, *Death and Elizabethan Tragedy* (New York: Pageant Books, 1960), p. 3.

[4] Johan Huizinga, *The Waning of the Middle Ages* (New York: Doubleday Anchor Books, 1954), p. 138.

[5] William M. Bowsky, ed., *The Black Death: A Turning Point in History?* (New York: Holt, Rinehart and Winston, 1971), p. 1; cf.: Philip Ziegler, *The Black Death* (New York: Harper and Row, 1969).

[6] "At the close of the Middle Ages the whole vision of death may be summed up in the word *macabre,* in its modern meaning. Of course, this meaning is the outcome of a long process. But the sentiment it embodies, of something gruesome and dismal, is precisely the conception of death which arose during the last centuries of the Middle Ages. . . . Towards 1400 the conception of death in art and literature took a spectral and fantastic shape. A new and vivid shudder was added to the great primitive horror of death. The macabre vision arose from deep psychological strata of fear; religious thought at once reduced it to a means of moral exhortation. As such it was a great cultural idea, till in its turn it went out of fashion, lingering on in epitaphs and symbols in village cemeteries" (Huizinga, *op. cit.,* p. 144).

[7] For an informative discussion of these and other medieval and modern artistic images of death, see Carla Gottlieb, "Modern Art and Death," in *The Meaning of Death,* Herman Feifel, ed. (New York: McGraw-Hill, 1965), pp. 157–88.

[8] *Ibid.,* p. 172.

[9] Spencer, *op. cit.,* p. 23.

[10] This would hold true, though less dramatically so, even acknowledging the greater vulnerability to death among those in the lower socioeconomic strata of society. See the World Health Organization's mortality study of 34 countries, published in July, 1972.

[11] Simone de Beauvoir, *The Coming of Age,* Patrick O'Brien, trans. (New York: G. P. Putnam's Sons, 1972), p. 1. For an enlightening look at the problems of old age in present day society, see pp. 216–77.

[12] Arnold Toynbee, *Man's Concern with Death* (New York: McGraw-Hill, 1968), p. 131.

[13] Peter Berger, *The Sacred Canopy* (New York: Doubleday, 1967), p. 137.

[14] Kastenbaum and Aisenberg, *op. cit.,* p. 208.

[15] Jessica Mitford, in her now famous indictment of the burial business, quotes a spokesman from the funeral industry who encourages his col-

leagues to "avoid using the word 'death' as much as possible, even sometimes when such avoidance may seem impossible; for example, a death
certificate should be referred to as a 'vital statistics form.' One should
speak not of the 'job' but rather of the 'call.' We do not 'haul' a dead
person, we 'transfer' or 'remove' him—and we do this in a 'service car,'
not a 'body car.' We 'open and close' his grave rather than dig and fill
it, and in it we 'inter' rather than bury him. This is done not in a grave-
yard or cemetery but rather in a 'memorial park.' The deceased is beauti-
fied, not with make-up, but with 'cosmetics.' Anyway he didn't die, he
'expired.' " (Jessica Mitford, *The American Way of Death* [Greenwich,
Conn.: Fawcett Publications, 1963], pp. 62–63).

[16] Geoffrey Gorer, *Death, Grief and Mourning* (New York: Doubleday,
1965), p. 128.

[17] *Ibid.*, p. 131.

[18] *Ibid.*, p. 128.

[19] *Ibid.*, p. 195. "While natural death . . . [has become] more and
more smothered in prudery, violent death has played an ever-growing
part in the fantasies offered to mass audiences—detective stories, thrillers,
Westerns, war stories, spy stories, science fiction, and eventually horror
comics" (p. 197).

[20] Berger, *op. cit.*, p. 52.

[21] Ladislaus Boros, *The Mystery of Death* (New York: Herder and
Herder, 1965), p. 141.

[22] Karl Rahner, *On the Theology of Death* (New York: Herder and
Herder, 1972), p. 34. Rahner goes on to add: "This end of man in
Paradise, this 'death' without dying, would have been a pure, apparent
and active consummation of the whole man from within, without death
in the proper sense, that is, without suffering from without any violent
dissolution of the actual bodily constitution" (pp. 34–35).

[23] Donal J. Dorr, "Death," in *Death and Hope,* Harry J. Cargas and
Ann White, eds. (New York: Corpus Books, 1970), p. 19.

[24] John Macquarrie, "True Life in Death," *Journal of Bible and Religion*
31 (1963), p. 201. It is particularly for this reason that the common
definition of death as the separation of the body and soul has been seen
as inadequate. "For it is absolutely silent about the characteristic feature
of death, that it is a human event concerning man as a whole and as a
spiritual person, an event which concerns his very essence." (Karl Rahner,
"Death," *Sacramentum Mundi,* vol. 2 [New York: Herder & Herder,
1968], p. 59).

[25] It is also worth noting that this positive approach to death appears
so conspicuously in the letters of Ignatius of Antioch. Cf. "The Letters

of Ignatius, Bishop of Antioch," in *Early Church Fathers,* Cyril Richardson, ed. (New York: Macmillan, 1970), pp. 74–120.

[26] Macquarrie, *op. cit.,* p. 202.

[27] Ignatius of Antioch to the Trallians, 9, in Richardson, *op. cit.,* p. 100.

[28] To this writer's knowledge, the only study devoted to Heidegger's treatment of death in both his early *and* his later works is that by James M. Demske, *Being, Man and Death: A Key to Heidegger* (Lexington, Ky.: The University Press of Kentucky, 1970). According to Demske, the other relatively few studies which have been devoted to the theme of death in Heidegger have been restricted to Heidegger's earlier works (pp. 7–8).

[29] *Ibid.,* p. 72.

[30] *Ibid.,* p. 26.

[31] Martin Heidegger, *Being and Time,* John Macquarrie and Edward Robinson, trans. (New York: Harper and Row, 1962), p. 294.

[32] *Ibid.*

[33] *Ibid.,* p. 307.

[34] Demske, *op. cit.,* p. 110.

[35] Heidegger, *op. cit.,* p. 477.

[36] *Ibid.,* p. 289.

[37] Demske, *Being, Man and Death,* p. 29.

[38] James M. Demske, "Heidegger: Wisdom as Death," *Continuum* 5 (1967), p. 509.

[39] *Ibid.,* p. 509.

[40] Macquarrie, *op. cit.,* p. 206.

[41] *Ibid.* This is a position in which Macquarrie is not alone. Writing in this same vein, Piet Schoonenberg states that this rather negative expression, "sinlessness, is not to be regarded as a 'programmed' incapacity to sin, but as an unfailing constancy in resisting the temptations by which . . . [he] was assaulted 'in every respect . . . as we are' (Heb. 4:15). . . . Temptations coming merely 'from without' and demanding no inward struggle would be consistent only with a humanity of Christ in which, as the Appolinarists held, the divine Logos replaced the human soul. Such temptation would not have been redemptive, given the nature of our own temptations" (Piet Schoonenberg, "Sin," *Sacramentum Mundi,* vol. 6, p. 92).

[42] It would seem that the New Testament uses the word "flesh" (*sarx*) in both a negative sense implying sin (e.g., Rom. 8:12), and in a neutral sense understood as man's way of being simply as man (e.g., Gal. 4:13; 2 Cor. 12:7; Rom. 8:9). For a fuller treatment of this, see John Macquarrie, *An Existentialist Theology: A Comparison of Heidegger and Bultmann* (New York: Harper Torchbooks, 1965), pp. 104–08; cf.: John

A. T. Robinson, *The Body: A Study in Pauline Theology* (London: SCM Press, 1966), pp. 11–33.

[43] Macquarrie, "True Life in Death," p. 206.

[44] Dorr, *op. cit.*, p. 12. Dorr continues: "All during life the process of self-creation is going on. Each free decision contributes to the total pattern, but no one decision is irrevocable in nature. There is always the possibility of a major change in direction, a 'conversion.' There is something tentative about each decision, since even the most fervent resolutions can be broken—and even in making them one recognizes that. But death changes the picture completely. Once a man dies, his decision is made. He has said his say. He has made himself. Without death, man is condemned to an eternity of *trying* to make up his mind, an eternity of tentatively taking up one direction or another. So unless death comes to man, there is no full exercise of freedom; for it is only in death that man can finally set the seal on what he wants to make of himself and his world. So while many existentialists hold that death deprives human life of its meaning, the Christian must say that death is a meaningful part of human life, and in fact, that death gives human life its meaning."

[45] Macquarrie, "True Life in Death," p. 205.

[46] Karl Rahner, *On the Theology of Death*, pp. 70–71.

[47] Michael Schmaus, "Death as Fulfillment," *Continuum* 5 (1967), p. 485.

[48] Rahner, *On the Theology of Death*, p. 69.

[49] William F. Lynch, *Images of Hope* (New York: New American Library, 1965), p. 210.

[50] *Ibid.*, pp. 211–12.

Contributors

BARBARA AGNEW, C.PP.S., is an assistant professor in the Department of Religious Studies at Villanova University, Pennsylvania.

SEELY BEGGIANI is rector of Our Lady of Lebanon Maronite Seminary in Washington, D.C., and a faculty member in the Religion and Religious Education Department at The Catholic University of America.

JAMES T. CONNELLY, C.S.C., teaches at King's College, Wilkes-Barre, Pennsylvania, and is writing a dissertation on neo-pentecostalism at the University of Chicago.

JOSEPH A. GRASSI is acting chairman of the Religious Studies Department at the University of Santa Clara, California.

JOHN A. GRAY teaches at Mercy College of Detroit, and is acting chairman of the Religious Studies Department.

MONIKA KONRAD HELLWIG has written extensively on contemporary theological issues. She teaches at Georgetown University, Washington, D.C., as an associate professor in the Theology Department.

ROBERT KRESS is a chaplain at the Newman Center and an associate professor of Philosophy and Religion at the University of Evansville in Indiana.

JOSEPH A. LA BARGE teaches at Bucknell University in Lewisburg, Pennsylvania, as an assistant professor in the Department of Religion.

THOMAS M. MCFADDEN (editor) is chairman of the College Theology Society's publications committee. He teaches

231

at Saint Joseph's College in Philadelphia, Pennsylvania.

ANDREW MALONEY teaches at the University of Saint Thomas in Houston, Texas, as an assistant professor within the Theology Department.

WILLIAM E. MAY teaches Christian ethics in the Department of Religion and Religious Education at The Catholic University of America, Washington, D.C.

BERNARD P. PRUSAK is an assistant professor and chairman of the graduate committee in the Department of Religious Studies at Villanova University, Pennsylvania.

C. GILBERT ROMERO is completing his dissertation in Old Testament theology at Princeton Theological Seminary, New Jersey, and is a part-time member of the theology faculty at La Salle College, Philadelphia, Pennsylvania.

DATE DUE

GAYLORD			PRINTED IN U.S.A.